CREATING THE
VOLUN-CHEER FORCE

Rethinking the way we use volunteers in long-term care

PAUL P. FALKOWSKI, PH.D.

Paul P. Falkowski, Ph.D.
VolunCheerLeader LLC
PO Box 54688
Philadelphia, PA 19148
www.voluncheerleader.com
Ordering Information: For details, contact the author at the address above.

Editors: Mary Hoekstra, writeandeditright5@gmail.com,
Mary Falkowski

Interior and cover designs by Najdan Mancic
Printed in the United States of America by BookBaby,
Pennsauken Township, NJ

Library of Congress Control Number: 2019911421
Falkowski, Paul P.

Creating a Volun-Cheer Force: rethinking the way we use volunteers in long-term care / Paul P. Falkowski.

Includes bibliographical references and index.
ISBN 978-1-7339394-2-3 (pbk.)

Dedication

———

This book is dedicated to the hundreds of wonderful people I met during my visits to nursing homes. Through their shared wisdom and life experiences, I learned that our relationships to friends and family is the most valuable gift of all.

Contents

———

Acknowledgments

———————

WRITING THIS BOOK was not the effort of one person but rather a network of peers, friends, and family coming together to contribute their thoughts and ideas culminating in what I hope will inspire new ways of thinking about volunteers in long-term care communities.

First and foremost, I want to thank the choir members who suggested that we go to the local nursing home to sing Christmas carols. It was at that nursing home that the seed for working with older adults was planted.

Second, I want to recognize Dr. Chuck Powell, Department of Gerontology, the University of Nebraska at Omaha for encouraging me to come back to school to earn a graduate certificate in gerontology that resulted in a doctorate in gerontology. Moreover, thank you to all the faculty and staff at UNO who have supported me in this venture.

I am very grateful to Mary Hoekstra for her expert editing and her patience with me through that process and to Najdan Mancic for his beautiful book design. I also want to thank Patrick Alyward at BookBaby for answering my thousands of questions while guiding me through the process of getting this book into your hands.

One of things I most enjoy about working in the field of aging are friendships and input from some very remarkable people like Gary George, Karen Kelly, Mary Parker, Rachel Brandenburg, Dr. Allen Power, Daniella Greenwood, Judy Sealer, Jill Woodward, Dr. Amy Hanson, Syrelle Bernstein, Janis Sternhill, Sabrina Teles, Cameo Rogers, Joy Rich, Lisa Hayes, and Jean Reiner, all providing valuable insight as I developed this book. There are so many more that I could list.

Finally, I want to thank my wife Mary, and my children Steven and Katherine for their loving support throughout this journey.

What If?

---

*"If you can imagine it, you can achieve it. If
you can dream it, you can become it.*

—**William Arthur Ward**

EVERYONE SEEMS FOCUSED on the aging of 80 million Baby Boomers, but I am not hearing much conversation about the 88 million Millennials who will begin turning 65 years of age just as the last of the Boomers are turning 85. The growth of this aging American population means, somewhere around the middle of the 21st century, there will be some 100 million people over the age of 65 who, depending on their health status, may be looking for long-term care services. In the meantime, there will be some 2.2 million openings for professional caregivers and managers. So, while I do not want to create a "doom and gloom" message, I do see an excellent opportunity to expand community involvement. I do not believe we can afford to ignore any possible resource.

Robust volunteer programs for nursing homes and other communities where older adults live become great recruiting tools, as well. I got into this world because I started as a volunteer. I do not think my experience is unique. Once I saw the need and learned how I could contribute to the lives of the people living and working in nursing homes, I left behind other aspirations for this one.

Over the years, I have met many people who have had similar experiences. They started as a nursing home volunteer and went on to become administrators, nurses, social workers, activity directors and so on. Create a great volunteer program, and you open the doors for new workers.

I love to watch old science fiction movies, particularly those that deal with space travel. I chuckle as the little model rocket, dangling from what I believe is a clear thread, seems to valiantly whisk its human passengers to some distant planet. The spacecraft was meant to be so sophisticated yet lacked any semblance of grace as it bounced along through the darkness of space.

If only the creators of those early 20th century movies could see where rockets are taking us now. In the same vein, I would love to see the Wright brothers' reactions as they witness the flyover of a super-sonic fighter jet or a two-level super airliner, outfitted with onboard apartments on the upper level. I am sure they would be amazed. Dreaming of and pursuing space travel and flight have brought about some fantastic results. Moreover, that brings me to my vision—my dream. From a movie script to the physics of space flight, all projects begin with a vision.

What if I told you there are people in your city, your town, your neighborhood, who have reached mid-career or are nearing retirement, and are looking for meaningful ways to give back to their communities? They are passionate about serving older adults living in long-term care communities. They are eager to learn new skills and they are willing to endure stringent vetting and training protocols. They want to be a reliable support for your staff and the people who live in your nursing home…and they are there, waiting for you to open your doors to them.

With this book, I'm sharing with you what I have learned through more than 25 years of experience in vetting and training volunteers for nursing homes; I'm sharing the research that supports this dream—this vision, of available, reliable volunteers waiting to give their time, talents and knowledge as adjuncts to your nursing home staff.

I encourage you to read this book cover-to-cover and to consider the potential value of a well-trained volunteer force, not only to provide meaningful relationships with the people who live in your nursing home, but also to provide positive relationships with your staff. This volunteer force can learn and perform the non-technical tasks of resident care, while freeing your professional and highly trained staff to engage in the technical jobs only they can do.

If contemplating that possibility, I would ask myself, as Litwak (1985) asked, "Is using highly trained nursing staff to complete nontechnical tasks such as dressing someone a good use of resources?" Can a nurse or a nurse aide take the time each morning to ask and discuss with each resident what they would like to wear, how they would like their hair combed and what they would like for breakfast? In the current climate, the answer is likely "No."

What could be an opportunity for volunteers who would provide person-centered care through conversation, learning more about a person, and respecting their wishes, would not the likely reply of your nursing staff be, "I have ten people to get dressed and ready for the day. I don't have time to chit-chat. I have a job to do." And before we go forward, please do not think for a minute that my opinion of direct-care and support staff is anything but the very best. In my years of experience, the majority of people I have met, i.e., nurses and nurse aides, are trying to provide excellent care in a system that works against them. The reality is, there are too few people on staff, so those who are working race from one end of their shift to the other end.

I have organized this book by looking first at my own experience: I started as a volunteer. I like to tell my students that I went to a nursing home to play music for the people living there.

I never came out and I wound up with a doctorate in gerontology. When people volunteer in a nursing home, the experience can have far-reaching effects on them. And this is my point: To also provide meaningful support to the people who live and work in your long-term care community; a well-managed volunteer program can become a conduit for recruiting workers. Over the years, several of the volunteers I've recruited and trained went on to become nurse aides, activity directors, and even bookkeepers in nursing home communities. One of the volunteers I trained left her corporate position as a controller to become bookkeeper at a nursing home in her hometown. The time I spent in nursing homes radically changed my perceptions of nursing homes and of older adults. Now, I tell people that I am like the moth drawn to the candlelight; I cannot stay away.

To write Chapter Two, I interviewed people who volunteered or worked in nursing homes before the Omnibus Reconciliation Budget Act of 1987 (OBRA 1987), a law that, in addition to balancing the United States budget, included the Nursing Home Reform Act (NHRA). At that time in the history of nursing homes, there was a drastic need for regulations to control spending and to ensure the safety of the people living in these places. I suggest, however, that we threw the baby out with the bathwater. When talking with the people I interviewed for the chapter, I was amazed to hear the passion they had for older adults who could most clearly recall events that took place decades ago. I was also surprised to learn that in some communities nurses were training volunteers and had fully integrated the volunteer and professional staff. The nurses were grateful for the help.

Reading regulations is not one of my favorite pastimes, but in Chapter Three, I review the Nursing Home Reform Act to describe how the new laws impacted the operations of nursing homes and how they impacted the people living in and working in these places. Also, I discuss the evolution of long-term care, and the emergence of assisted living and efforts, like the Eden Alternative and Green Houses developed by Dr. William (Bill) Thomas, that will and are transforming long-term care.

In Chapter Four, I present what I learned from Daniella Greenwood, as well as what I learned from Dr. Thomas Kitwood and Dr. Allen Power, regarding recognizing, respectively, that there is more to giving care than just meeting the physical needs of a person; and that the conversation about meeting those needs must move to "relational care" or creating "authentic partnerships;" (DuPuis, Gillies, Carson, Whyte, Genoe, & Loiselle, et al. 2012; Power 2017a). Again, I contend that volunteers, vetted and well-trained, are in the perfect position to provide that level of intimate interaction. The volunteer, in gaining this level of insight into someone's needs, can help inform the staff and the care planning process.

For sure, there are challenges to creating this level of what I call "super" volunteers. In my conversations with people working in the field, I have identified five main objections in Chapter Five for *not* pursuing robust volunteer programs. When one weighs those objections against the future of an increasingly aging population that will need long-term care, and the daunting challenges of hiring and retaining staff, we can ill afford to ignore the "altruistic" motivations and devotion of the people in our communities who possess a passion for caring for older adults.

Several organizations recognize and have created programs that take advantage of and maximize volunteer potential. I've devoted Chapter Six to highlighting groups such a Baycrest in Toronto, Kristiansund kommune in Norway, Elizabeth Knox Hospital and Nursing Home in New Zealand for starters.

Shifting a paradigm is no easy task, but that is precisely what needs to happen when it comes to how volunteers are viewed and used in long-term care support systems. In Chapter Seven, I share my own experiences with developing the vetting and training program as well as the five key ingredients that "super" volunteers possess, starting with "Community." We encourage people to "age in place" but what if the "community" ignores or rejects the older population? "Super" volunteers understand that "community" comprises everyone, including the older adults living in that community, and additionally, the people who live in a nursing home near them.

For Chapter Eight, I present the interviews with three "super" volunteers. I selected them because they truly exemplify and fully represent the term "super." Joy Rich's sensitivity and creativity opened the doors for her to create a wonderful program. Sabrina Teles, a Baycrest volunteer, trained in cutting edge programs and Lisa Hayes, the senior instructional designer for her company, found that volunteering in a nursing home was a way she could exercise the tenets of her faith, i.e., helping those in need.

Creating a *Super Volun-Cheer Force* requires setting the bar high for volunteer programs. Great programs are well thought out, planned, and executed under the direction of a paid, professional director of volunteers. While Chapter Nine is not a step-by-step recipe for creating a great volunteer program, it does lay out the foundational elements of what a volunteer program needs in order to be successful. Those elements are research-based, given my research, my experiences and the interviews I conducted with professional directors of volunteers.

Finally, I've tried to avoid projecting the "crisis" mentality regarding nursing home communities, but in Chapter Ten, I suggest we must face the future head-on. We are going to need a lot of professional caregivers to meet the demand for long-term care.

Before we get into the process of creating a "Volun-Cheer-Force," let me tell you a bit of my story.

CHAPTER ONE

A Little History

Then the Grinch thought of something he hadn't before!
What if Christmas, he thought, doesn't come from a store.
What if Christmas...perhaps...means a little bit more!

—DR. SEUSS, "HOW THE GRINCH STOLE CHRISTMAS!"

THE FIRST TIME I took our choir into a nursing home, it never occurred to me that 30 years later, I would write a book advocating for "super" volunteers to supplement nursing home staff. As with many church and civic groups, the holiday season still brings out some of our best behaviors, one of which was taking a group to the local nursing home to sing Christmas carols for the "old people" living at the "old folks" home. That is just what happened to me. I have since corrected my language and understanding of long-term care, as I know you have, as well.

Let me explain. Just before Christmas, 1986, the choir director at my church resigned. The following Sunday, our pastor announced the resignation and pleaded for help, "If anyone knows anything about music, we could sure use your help!" I cannot sing to save my life, but because of my training, (my bachelor's degree is in music performance), I can read musical scores and conduct. I responded to the pastor's plea and managed to get the choir through that Christmas season, but not before an event during that time changed the direction of my life.

It was several weeks before Christmas and I was busy preparing music for the choir to sing during the remainder of the holiday season. During one of our choir rehearsals, a member of the choir suggested that the choir go to the nearby nursing home to perform our Christmas music. I agreed, though I had no idea what to expect and had never been inside a nursing home. Nevertheless, I called the nursing home close to the church and asked if we could come to their "facility" to sing for their residents. The person with whom I spoke was the activities director, who emphatically said, "Yes!" On the Sunday afternoon scheduled for our visit, the choir and I loaded into the church van and set off for the nursing home.

When we arrived, a member of the staff ushered us to an activity area that served several purposes, one of which was a place to hold chapel services. The room was well-equipped with a stage for an electronic organ, a piano and a podium. The stage was large enough to accommodate the fifteen choir members and myself. People, staff, families and their loved ones gathered in the chapel.

When everyone was seated and ready, I motioned to the accompanist to begin and the choir began to sing. Although I do not remember which Christmas carol we sang first, and I had my back to the audience, I remember hearing the people singing behind me. I was curious to see them and turned to face the audience. For a moment, for me, time stood still. I was deeply moved by what I saw. There, sitting before us was a group of frail older adults, some wrapped in blankets, some dressed in very plain clothes, most in wheelchairs, and most with gray hair or balding heads. It struck me hard that, despite their circumstances, they were smiling and they were singing. Seeing them filled with such joy pricked my heart. These words flooded my mind, "...pure and undefiled religion is this, to visit the widow and orphan in their distress..." It was obvious that while we were there singing, we not only helped the residents celebrate the holiday, but we also brought them a deep sense of joy and meaning. Afterward, on our way back to the church, I said to the choir, "I think we should do this more often and not just at Christmas." I was hooked.

For the next several years, on a Sunday afternoon after church each month, the choir and I traveled to a nursing home to sing whatever songs we had performed in church that morning. It was an excellent experience for all of us, and so much so for me that I began making these visits on my own. I play three saxophones: the soprano, alto and tenor. I pulled together a 40-minute program of familiar songs and began scheduling visits to the 20 or so communities in my city of Omaha. As time passed, my visits became more frequent; soon, I was making appointments daily, all the while observing the dynamics of each nursing home in which I performed.

About six months into making personal visits, I received a letter from an activities director of a nursing home in Manilla, Iowa. In her letter, she said she had heard about what I was doing in Omaha and asked if I would be willing to come to her facility and play for the people there. At that time, and without our present GPS, I had no idea where Manilla, Iowa was. From the map of Iowa, I learned it was about 100 miles northeast of Omaha. I called the activities director and explained I was willing to come to her facility once, but could not promise I'd be able to make regular visits. Working together, we scheduled a day for me to come. By then, I had learned the best time to visit nursing homes was in the afternoon. So, on the day I was to go to Manilla, I packed up my gear and started around 11:30 a.m., anticipating a two-hour trip. To my surprise, it was a beautiful drive through the Loess Hills of Iowa. It was quite scenic and relaxing and along the way, I couldn't help but wonder what was in store for me in Manilla. When I arrived at Manilla Manor, the activities director, the care staff and the residents received me warmly. They were surprised at the amount of gear I had brought with me; i.e., a public address system and not one, but three saxophones! They were fascinated by the horns and all the gear. They wanted to touch them, and I let them do this while I explained the names of the instruments and gave them a little history concerning each one.

Once again, however, as I played familiar songs, I was deeply moved by what I saw and heard. Seeing their smiles and hearing not only the voices of the residents, but those of the staff as well, once again, it seemed time stood still. As the program progressed, the room filled to the point that I was reasonably sure nearly everyone, residents and staff alike, was in the dining room with me. It was a lovely time. People were singing, some were smiling, and some had a few tears in their eyes too.

One female resident said, "These are not tears of sadness but tears of great joy." When it was time for me to leave, I already knew I would be coming back. I had two hours of driving home to reflect on this decision.

When I arrived home that evening, I returned to my desk where the map still lay open to Iowa. I placed my finger on Manilla and, remembering the day's events and knowing how much my visit meant to them, I re-confirmed the decision I had made earlier in the day. Driving the 100 miles or so was not that difficult and I could still be home in time for dinner.

Using a piece of string and a pencil, I drew a circumference around Omaha, using Manilla as the radius. I had defined my territory. Over the next few weeks, I learned that there were some 170 nursing homes inside that circle, not counting assisted living or independent living communities. It became clear to me just how many people lived in all the types of communities for older adults. My heart went out to them all.

Next, I called each nursing home or facility, introduced myself, and scheduled a visit. I became so busy that my wife, Mary, began helping me by making those calls, keeping track of my schedule and sending out posters announcing my play dates. Soon, I was traveling every day of the week, logging 35,000 to 40,000 miles each year, but I was never more than 100 miles from home. I was becoming a student of long-term care.

During those visits, I talked with the care staff. I wanted to glean as much information as possible from them about what it was like to work in a nursing home. I heard their needs, what challenges they faced and what I could do to support them.

When I asked the care staff members what the residents needed, almost without exception, they told me, "one-on-one" visits. They needed a friend. They needed to feel like someone cared about them. This message came through both the staff and residents to whom I spoke.

Once I asked an activities director, "How many volunteers do you need?"

She immediately shot back, "140!"

Shocked, I asked, "Well how many people live here?"

She smiled and said, "140!"

While talking with, an older woman residing in one of the communities I visited, she observed, "I have a lot of people around, nurses and staff but there is no one here just for me." With this consistent feedback, I realized everyone living in a nursing home needs to feel someone cares about them, and that they are not forgotten. At the same time, each resident needed to care for someone, too.

They needed meaningful relationships. Everyone needs a friend, a companion, a confidant. Without those intimate relationships, people feel alone, forgotten, useless, as though they no longer have purpose and no reason to wake up the next day.

I observed and learned many people living in nursing homes do not have that person with whom they can share their life, their stories, their feelings, even their secrets. In fact, less than half of all nursing home residents had that person, who, as one resident said to me was, "…someone that is here just for me."

Research shows that this lack of intimacy leads to depression, out-of-character responses, unnecessary call lights, premature death and even attempted and successful suicides. Statistics for attempted suicides in nursing homes are difficult to come by; often they are not reported or it is difficult to determine whether the attempt was intentional. Mezuk, Lohman, Leslie, & Powell (2015) reported the rate for successful suicides in nursing homes is 14.16 out of 100K. I can imagine an older person thinking, "What a sad ending to a person's life story. I lived into old age only to discover I have no purpose."

Learning and affirming how important on-going relationships are to the well-being of each nursing home resident, I found it ironic that I de-emphasized my music performances and instead turned my attention and efforts to educating people about this need for companionship so many residents expressed to me. I learned the impact that one-on-one, regular visits can have on people living in nursing homes. I did all that I could to encourage people to join me when I visited the people in nursing homes. I started with the people at my church and expanded my outreach to other churches. Finally, I expanded my effort to reach each city in which the communities existed, and anyone else who would listen to me. During 1999, I recruited my first volunteer, Dave. He had attended one of my presentations and was responding to my pleas for help.

During my initial interview with Dave, I explained what was happening in nursing homes and how much of an impact he could have on the residents, as well as staff. For training, I had him read two books: *Another Country* by Mary Pipher, Ph.D. and *Compas-*

sion by Henri Nouwen, and then write two book reports. Of course Dave fulfilled that assignment.

For those of you not familiar with *Another Country*, it is a collection of interviews with nursing home residents, care staff and the families of loved ones living in a nursing home. *Another Country* offers valuable insights into the world of long-term care from each stakeholder's perspective.

In *Compassion*, Nouwen (1983) draws the reader's attention to thinking about what compassion is and asking themselves whether they are compassionate or competitive. I had people read this book to introduce the notion that the people living in nursing homes were not our "target audience;" they were not there for us to fix, but instead, they were human beings who needed someone to be present for them, to have the capacity to enter into their world; and to become their fellow sojourner.

I then called the activities director at a nursing home with which I had a good rapport and announced with some glee, "I think I have a volunteer for you!" We set up a time for Dave's initial visit to the nursing home; I would accompany Dave on this first visit to introduce him to the activities director and help him break the ice.

When Dave and I arrived at the nursing home, the activities director came out to greet us and I introduced Dave to her. With a big smile, she said to Dave, "Come in, I'd like you to call Bingo for us today!" To my surprise, I watched a wave of terror wash across Dave's face. I realized and was fairly certain that Dave had never played Bingo, let alone called a game. Off they went to the dayroom. I waved goodbye to Dave, thinking, *This is a disaster. I'll never see him again.* Three weeks passed with no word from Dave, so I was fairly certain he was long gone. However, one day the telephone rang, and it was Dave; I could tell he was upset.

Through a quavering voice, he said, "I almost quit today because I couldn't see the spiritual value of calling bingo. As I was leaving for the last time, just as my hand hit the push bar of the door, one of the residents, an older woman, grabbed my arm and said, 'Thanks, Dave for coming. You're like family to us now.' I broke down at the door. I went back into the dayroom and sat down. The residents, [seeing Dave's tears], couldn't understand why I was so upset and so they gathered around me, to comfort and nurture me."

I was in complete shock as I listened to Dave's story; he called Bingo every Wednesday for five years. Hearing what happened to Dave, I realized people living in nursing homes had something to offer the volunteer, starting with giving him or her a new perspective on what life is all about.

Over the years, I have heard similar stories from volunteers. Their visits to nursing homes had a significant impact on the volunteers as much as they did on the residents they were visiting. Clearly, those visits were a two-way street.

One volunteer said to me, "I talk to my wife a little differently, and I hug my kids a little more." I know this from personal experience as well; there have been many times when I felt I was receiving much more than I was giving. While the volunteer intended to cheer someone up and restore to that resident a sense of being loved and cared for, the resident reciprocated by offering unconditional love and wisdom to the volunteer. Eventually, I concluded it was entirely possible we needed them more than they needed us. We need to hear their stories and to learn, among other things, that time is precious; we need to face the fact that our lives are finite.

In the beginning stages of recruiting volunteers, I assumed the nursing homes would provide in-depth volunteer training, so I did not feel the need to expand the training I was giving my volunteers.

I recruited the volunteer, gave them some background information, then placed them in a nursing home. It became increasingly apparent after some time passed that some nursing homes were not providing adequate training for their volunteers. In fact, on several occasions, after having recruited someone, building them up for this experience, and arriving at the nursing home, they would discover that it seemed as if no one cared they were there, let alone providing training for them. Several volunteers I sent out told me they were quite disappointed and would not be returning to the nursing home. Hearing their disappointment was troubling for me. I knew the staffing shortage was reaching a point where, in some cases, the nursing home could not adequately support a volunteer program. At this point, I knew I had to make a change.

During 2010, I temporarily stopped recruiting volunteers. I knew I had to expand our training to the point that when the volunteer arrived at the nursing home, they would be thoroughly prepared for their volunteer experience. Based on the feedback I garnered from administrators, directors of nursing, nurse aides and with the help of a terrific friend, Andrew Dungan, Ed.D., I wrote a comprehensive training program. It took the better part of the year, conducting focus groups and personal interviews, and reading and researching the literature. From all this input, we developed a 16-hour training program that prepared the volunteer for nursing home experiences.

The training included both classroom theory concerning the aging process, myths about aging, the various levels of care provided by nursing homes, and communication techniques. Next came hands-on training. Care staff who completed the training stated it was more training than they received on the job. Finally, in November 2010, I graduated our first class of volunteers. I didn't realize it then, but I had just produced the first of what I now call "super" volunteers; there are many of them.

I had raised the bar high. Our vetting process included conducting background checks, requiring three written letters of reference, scheduling personal interviews and when they finished those tasks, they were invited to attend the volunteer training. At first, I wasn't sure if anyone would be willing to endure, or even survive this process, but to my amazement, people did respond, and they responded with enthusiasm! I soon learned setting the bar high meant we would attract people who were willing and could jump that high. Admittedly and right up front, the attrition rate was about 50-60%. My rationale for this was and remains simple: Why send out people who are not fully committed to the cause?

Nursing homes need to be able to rely on committed people, including volunteers. Nursing home staff has to be sure they can depend on the volunteers I send to them. Therefore, I've learned to invest my time and effort only in those people who demonstrate a clear, authentic commitment to serving people living and working in nursing homes. Without exaggeration, I can say the people who complete the vetting process and the volunteer training are exceptional. They are highly committed, highly motivated people, with the intellectual capacity and desire to learn new skills. Clearly, they are not doing this for financial gain; they are completing training and honoring their assignments because they have a real passion, a sincere concern for and an obligation to serving older adults.

Now, almost a decade later, I have trained several hundred such people, and every one of them is extraordinary. They are remarkable in their commitment and exceptional in their ability to serve. Every training session is a thrill for me, as I have the opportunity to equip one more remarkable person. I believe there are many, many more people in our communities like those I have found. In reality, many of them found me. In fact, in the following chapters, you will read about organizations who have discovered the same thing

I have; i.e., give great people the opportunity to do great things and they will. With the genuine and growing need for long-term care staffing, we cannot afford to ignore any resource available to us that can improve our chances of providing the quality care that we desire to give. "Super" volunteers are one of those resources to discover, identify and utilize. I know all nursing home directors and staff want to give their residents "person-centered" care. "Super" volunteers can do that. Why? Because they have the "luxury of time" (Gross, 1961).

Like Dave's story of transformation, my own story is transformational. When I started in 1992, I had no idea what long-term care was, what the issues were, or that one day I would be advocating for robust volunteer programs. But after seeing what happened to Dave and all our volunteers and seeing the impact they were making on the people they were visiting, I clearly knew what my vision and mission were.

My idea was to discover volunteers as a work-ready resource to enhance the quality of life in nursing homes. My purpose was to identify the skills volunteers would need in the nursing home and then to develop training programs to prepare volunteers so when they arrived at the nursing home, they could hit the ground running. I was creating the "super" volunteer, the "trusted" volunteer, the "Volun-Cheer Force."

I am well-aware of the challenges I face in promoting this idea. For that reason, I wrote this book to encourage you, the delegator, the administrator, the policymaker, to not just turn away, shaking your head, but rather seriously consider what I am presenting to you.

The following chapters clearly show several issues. First, the idea of expanding the role of the volunteer is already happening. The concept of supplementing staff with trained volunteers is not unique to me. I present examples of how this is working very well for other long-term care providers. Second, I am not promoting the idea of replacing paid professional staff with volunteers. We need well-trained professional caregivers too! But we don't have nearly enough to do the job, so integrating a well-trained cadre of volunteers to provide a "helping hand" to supplement the professional caregivers is a must. As great as the "super" volunteers are, and as well trained as they are and will be, they cannot provide the technical services and care only professional staff has been trained to provide. Volunteers are not a substitute for professional staff, nor am I advocating for that! However, it is clear there will not be nearly enough professional staff to provide quality care to individuals entering and living in long-term care communities. Therefore, we cannot afford to ignore any possible support resource.

The "super" volunteer will lift some of the workload, but not all of it; they cannot. What the "super" volunteer can do is free up time for the professional staff to provide the technical care only they can provide. Finally, I hope the following chapters will inspire you, and even challenge you, to join me in bringing together the long-term care providers who embrace the viability of this idea, and to take the "super" volunteer even one step further and create the "credentialed" volunteer. But before we look at that, let's take a quick look back to see how we might have "thrown the baby out with the bath water."

CHAPTER TWO

A Little More History

―――――

*Don't toss out something that is valuable in your effort
to discard the undesirable. To put it more succinctly,
don't throw the baby out with the bath water.*

―**PAUL FALKOWSKI**

T HE ADOPTION OF the Omnibus Budget Reconciliation
Act (OBRA) 1987 included the Nursing Home Reform Act,
(NHRA). The NHRA brought about significant and positive changes to the way nursing homes were regulated, operated and staffed. If
there was any hope of using volunteers in expanded support roles in
nursing homes, the NHRA all but eliminated that possibility. His-
torically, operators and owners have looked with a wary eye at the use
of volunteers to provide care. As early as 1961, Anne Gross, director
of volunteer services at Mt. Zion Hospital and Medical Center, San
Francisco, advocating for the increased use of volunteers wrote in
Why Nursing Homes Need Volunteers:

> *Perhaps proprietors who know nothing of volunteer activities are
> suspicious of inviting outsiders in; perhaps they fear discord be-
> tween volunteers and paid staff; perhaps they fear volunteer in-
> volvement in the many senile complaints; perhaps they fear com-
> plications and bother from volunteer visits in an enterprise which
> has enough of its own complications and bother. (Gross, 1961)*

For me, the key word in her quote is "fear." Fear stifles innovation, stagnating the hope of finding new solutions. Rather than pursue new ideas and remedies, fear causes one to recoil, leaving only the option of retreating to a place of familiarity. The foundation for that place of familiarity, in this case, the prescribed role of volunteers, may have its roots in the evolution community organizations created in the late 19th century to address the social ills of that day.

In his book, *In the Shadow of the Poorhouse,* Katz (1996) details the process of providing aid to those who were living in poverty. Volunteers, or as they were called then, "friendly visitors" were to befriend those receiving assistance, to be their cheerleader, offering them primarily emotional support and acting as a liaison between them and the organization providing the support. In time, the thought process changed and from that emerged a new professional, the social worker. More than a friendly visit, what impoverished people needed was "an expert" who could guide the needy to a better place and establish the providing organization as a valuable resource for meeting their needs. And so, the volunteer, the "friendly visitor" was pushed into the background.

Of note to me was Katz's concluding comment about this paradigm shift. He wrote, "...any passion for social reform vanished..." (p. 171).

Passion. Volunteers bring more than just a *friendly visit;* they bring their passion with them. Motivated by a caring spirit, the volunteer brings an authentic empathy for the plight of those around them. Combining passion with quality training creates a new resource, what I would term as the "passionate volunteer expert." I am not saying that social workers or other care staff are not passionate about their work, I am saying that people who choose to freely give of their time and talent, because of their passion, should not be dismissed to merely marginal roles. Given the current climate in long-term care staffing, we can ill afford to turn away any source of support, to include volunteers.

As the 20th century progressed, the role of the volunteer continued to be viewed as non-critical; as a result, the stigma developed that volunteers were unreliable, unsustainable amateurs. That stigma remains cemented in the consciousness of the American people, specifically, in this instance, the owners and operators of nursing homes, including decision makers and policymakers.

More often than not, when I have the opportunity to address a group of managers and people from the medical profession concerning volunteers supplementing care staff, there are two immediate reactions from the group. Among the first reactions is: volunteers are not reliable, you cannot count on them, and they are apt to choose some more pleasant activity rather than fulfill their commitment to the nursing home. These reactions may accurately describe volunteer programs with volunteers who are not adequately screened, trained and managed by a professional volunteer manager. As a result, these programs falter and stumble, eventually failing or, at the very least, creating more headaches for the staff. In other words, low expectations from staff and professionals set the volunteer program to fail. What I have learned is, you put a professional volunteer manager in place and set your expectations high. In other words, raise the bar!

Before the Nursing Home Reform Act (NHRA, 1987), volunteers were available to provide a variety of meaningful and vital supporting functions to nursing home residents and staff alike. My interviews with staff and volunteers working and volunteering before the NHRA revealed that volunteers were helping with just about every aspect of nursing home operations. They were assisting residents in getting dressed, providing feeding assistance, spending one-on-one time with residents, and most importantly, they were freeing the professional staff to do the more complex levels of care.

According to the people I interviewed, the relationships between volunteers and staff were excellent. There are several current and excellent examples operating today where volunteers are supporting professional staff in critical and meaningful ways as they did before NHRA, (see Chapter Six).

From the interviews I conducted, people who volunteered in nursing homes before the enactment of the NHRA remember how the staff embraced the volunteers. The professional staff recognized that this was a potential permanent worker who would likely go on to become a professional caregiver. This was the case for one of the people I interviewed. As a young person, she hoped to become a doctor one day. She had an authentic passion for helping people and in particular people living in nursing homes. During the school year, she would volunteer on the weekends without fail; during the summer she was at the nursing home every day of the week offering her help. When I asked her what sorts of help she was providing, her response caught me off guard. The staff, knowing she wanted to go on to become a professional, taught her how to change linens, bathe people, change diapers, provide feeding assistance, work in the kitchen and even taught her how to perform some of the more difficult tasks, involving exchanging external male catheters, removing impacted stools and administering enemas. She told me, "It was phenomenal the things that I was allowed to do because I demonstrated I could do them. I could take vitals because I knew how to do that. They taught me how to do that, and I was doing it because I wanted to." Once again, we see her passion, commitment, and conscientiousness which are among the qualities that "super" volunteers have.

Now before you scream, be assured I am not proposing or advocating for volunteers to do such things today. What I am offering is this: there are people in our towns and cities who possess a similar authentic passion, a high level of commitment and, similar to the young woman volunteer, may be considering a career in healthcare. We have severely restricted what volunteers can and cannot do, based on the negative stereotypes of volunteers coupled with our fears of liability; this is what Dr. Allen Power refers to as "surplus safety" (2017a). In the nursing home field, we are not affording quality people, and possibly potential professional care-givers, the opportunities to experience what it means to work in a nursing home alongside professional staff in supportive roles. In this particular case, this volunteer's experience was evidence of how rewarding it could be to work in a nursing home. She admitted the work was not easy, but she added that the rewards she was receiving counter-balanced the challenges of the work. She did not become a doctor, but she did become a nurse.

Some fifty years later, she is still working with older adults in long-term care communities. She described her early days of vol-unteering as being, "…wonderful and that it was a privilege to be allowed to do this kind of stuff. I was incredibly grateful that I was trusted to do this. I learned a lot about mortality and loving people…" Would her story have been the same if the staff had relegated her to calling Bingo once a week? When I asked her this question, she said, "If they had just said, 'Well you can call bingo or wipe down tables,' I'm not sure I would have stayed as long as I did. But because I got to do meaningful work and I knew it made a difference, [I stayed]. I remember we had one resident who just needed someone to sit with him and I would be one of the people who would do that. It was significant at the time."

People are looking for meaningful volunteer experiences and they want to know they are making a real difference. Also, they are learning valuable life lessons, such as the reality that living in a nursing home could be a possible future for them. It leads us to take an inventory of how we are using our time and who are the people with whom we want to be connected. As I discuss in Chapter Seven, there are various levels of volunteer opportunities.

What I am proposing here is the "super" volunteer who wants more than just a casual visit. The "super" volunteer is looking for a meaningful opportunity where they know they are making a real difference. The young woman who became a nurse in a nursing home setting was a "super" volunteer. She was highly committed to the nursing home. She was reliable, showing up consistently from day-to-day and week-to-week. She was willing and wanting to learn new skills. She recognized that being given this level of responsibility was a privilege for which she was grateful. This level of volunteering, these "volunteers," if presented with the opportunity, can provide significant staff support that goes directly to the quality of care, quality of life and even staff retention. When the professional staff experiences this level of support, they too experience a lift and a sense of mastery. Experiencing the volunteer's passion and commitment reminds the professional caregiver why they got into the business of caring for people. It stirs their passion for caring. "I never saw a volunteer hurt a patient." That observation comes from a state surveyor recalling her days before the NHRA.

As far as increasing community engagement, the state surveyor talked about observing an "amazing" example of community support. The nursing home needed chart racks and reached out to the high school shop class. The students came to the nursing home, took measurements, built the racks and then installed them. Students during prom season would come to the nursing home and conduct a "prom parade." The parade became an annual ritual, and as a result of this and other community involvement activities, the older adults living in the nursing home were "100 percent fully engaged in what was going on in the community." For a retiring local barber, the nursing home staff took many of the residents downtown to his retirement celebration. "It was the whole community that embraced these older adults." Another example of this kind of community engagement involved the women of a nursing home being taken to a county fair to be pie judges. These are examples of communities fully embracing their local nursing home. With this, I will argue that expanding community engagement in the life of the nursing home not only benefits the residents, but it raises the level of accountability that the nursing home staff has to the community.

While these two examples of community engagement were rural settings, this level of community involvement is even more critical in urban environments. However, many of the people living in urban nursing homes may come to their nursing homes already "disenfranchised." In the rural settings, people may have been more likely to be members of churches, have had the benefit of local extension clubs and auxiliaries that would assist at the nursing home, and would have been more visible to the community. Much of this disconnection in the urban setting can be addressed by administrators aggressively making attempts to engage their surrounding community more fully. There are examples of nursing homes where this is already happening. Tabitha Health in Lincoln, Nebraska is an excellent example of this. There is a full-time director of volunteers on staff, along with a full-time volunteer coordinator. They manage some 1,000 volunteers serving in a variety of roles to include delivering meals through Meals on Wheels. Increasing community engagement raises awareness of the aging process while mitigating negative images of the nursing home.

I believe this excerpt from the UN Volunteers 2018 report re-enforces this idea:

Volunteerism strengthens local ownership, solidarity and inclusive participation, and it allows for swift responses to proximate crises. At the same time, under certain conditions volunteerism can be exclusive, burdensome, short-term and of limited effectiveness. This potential duality of volunteerism means that governments and development partners have an important role to play in maximizing volunteerism's positive contributions. Stakeholders must be mindful not to partner with volunteers as a source of cheap labour but rather would be well advised to nurture volunteerism as an attribute of resilient communities. This can be done through developing an ecosystem for resilient volunteering and creating new community partnerships with that work towards local resilience. (p. 14).

While interviewing nursing home care staff for this chapter, I learned that as long as the volunteers were properly trained, the care staff welcomed the idea of giving the volunteers more responsibility. The nurses and aides with whom I spoke talked about the incredible chore it was to meet the basic needs of the residents, and how volunteers picking up some of the non-medical tasks, such as dressing, grooming and feeding residents, would be so helpful in alleviating some of the burden now on care staff.

Once again, I am not advocating for going back to the "… good old days," when few regulations were governing the welfare of residents and allowing "untrained" people to do complicated medical tasks. What I am pointing out is, with proper training, i.e., training that "super" volunteers want, they can be a real and valuable asset to your long-term community (Damianakis, Wagner, Berstein, & Marziali, 2007; van der Ploeg, Mbakile, Genovesi, & O'Connor, 2012).

One of the persons I interviewed remembered the staff inviting her to have lunch with them, "…they always seemed to treat me like one of them…I never had a problem with the nurse aides…we ate together; we laughed together. When I think about that period, I think about how much I got out of it." She went on to talk about how her relationships with the residents were so meaningful. They would have long talks about their lives and their "take on things." She still remembers the woman who had multiple sclerosis, who could not move any part of her body, but had taught herself to paint holding the brush with her teeth.

My interviews with people who volunteered in nursing homes before the NHRA, in addition to daytime tasks, also revealed the fact that they would help at night, doing bed checks and assisting people to get changed for bed, "…because we liked them…" The volunteers wanted to help because they had become friends; one former volunteer pointed out that she would even go as far as to bathe residents. When I asked if they remembered any of the volunteers hurting or injuring the residents, they talked about how conscientious they were because these were people they had befriended.

Beyond helping the residents, a former volunteer, now retired, who went on to work in environmental services for over 19 years, recognized that volunteers should not be stripping and waxing floors, but they could help by emptying trash cans in the residents' rooms. She remembers helping to fold clothes in the laundry. She was not allowed to operate the machines, but she could help by folding clothes and then help the staff by delivering the clothes back to their owners. She also remembers helping to set tables in the dining room and of course assisting with activities. Now, years later, she has returned to volunteering with Foster Grandparents.

Finding people who had volunteered in nursing homes before the Nursing Home Reform Act was no small chore, but I believe, after several interviews, I could safely predict what the recurring themes would be in subsequent interviews. Those themes included, first, that the volunteer wanted to help and that they had a passion for being with and helping older adults. Their love and commitment allowed them to take on more responsibilities and to become a real asset to the care staff. Second, they had been considering careers in health care, and their experiences as nursing home volunteers gave them a preview of what it might be like to work in the field of long-term care. In all but one of the cases, the volunteer did go on to become either a nurse aide or a nurse. In one example, the volunteer went on to become a pastor and now serves as a chaplain in several long-term care communities.

Again, while I do not believe that strong volunteer programs will satisfy all staffing challenges, I do think that policies and regulations that govern volunteer involvement should be re-examined in light of the current circumstances. By not placing a renewed emphasis on community involvement through volunteerism, are we handicapping our efforts: 1) to provide quality of life for the residents; 2) to recruit new workers; and 3) to undo the ravages of poor care, inadequate funding, and resident abuse? Indeed, as a society, are we stifling the need to change our conceptualizations based on deeply embedded negative stereotypes of aging? While we certainly need policies and regulations to govern the care of one of our most precious resources, our elders, we want to be careful not to miss a great opportunity by stifling another valuable resource, i.e., the "super" volunteer.

CHAPTER THREE

Remember 1987?—We all walked like Egyptians!

"Slide your feet up the street bend your back, Shift your arm then you pull it back Life is hard you know (oh whey oh), So strike a pose on a Cadillac[1]"

TERRY WAITE IS taken captive. The stock market crashes. A gallon of gasoline costs eighty-seven cents. The world population approaches five billion. "Star Trek—The Next Generation" makes its debut. Alan Greenspan becomes chairman of the Federal Reserve Board, and disposable contact lenses become commercially available. The number one song was, Walk Like an Egyptian, recorded by The Bangles. Oh yes, and the Omnibus Budget and Reconciliation Act of 1987 (OBRA '87) was enacted. Within OBRA '87 was the Nursing Home Reform Act which appeared at Title IV, section C. The Nursing Home Reform Act (NHRA) brought about much-needed regulation of the nursing home industry, and an "industry" is exactly what it had become—and a lucrative industry at that.

---

[1] *"Walk Like an Egyptian"* a song recorded by the American band The Bangles, to become Billboard's number-one song of 1987.

As I discussed in Chapter Two, with the 1965 introduction of government-subsidized long-term care in the form of Medicaid, investors were well-aware of the financial potential for building nursing homes, getting them up and running and then selling them off for many times more than their original investment. The NHRA legislation brought about significant changes in the requirements for nursing home care. Nursing homes were now required to "provide care and services for each resident to attain or maintain his/her highest practicable level of physical, mental and psychosocial well-being." Vladeck (1980), covered the origins of the nursing home industry quite well in his book *Unloving Care: The Nursing Home Tragedy.* As such, I won't spend time recounting that history. Instead, I want to focus on the evolution of the nursing home and in particular the nursing home volunteer since the adoption of OBRA '87.

To begin, the areas addressed by OBRA '87 included, but were not limited to, the use of drugs to chemically restrain people, the use of physical restraints to control people, abuse and neglect committed by nursing home staff, and the rights of the people living in nursing homes to include having control over their care, among many other requirements. Raising the competency level of the direct care worker through mandatory training was now required, and volunteers were severely restricted in what they could do. Sorely needed policies and regulations meant to improve the care of older adults, inadvertently and severely limited a valuable resource for the nursing home—the volunteer.

This is the context for discussing the limits of the volunteer. In 1987, the reality of an aging population was still a distant issue of which most people in the United States were unaware. Baby Boomers were approaching midlife and life was good for most Boomers. They were pretty well convinced that they needn't concern themselves with aging for many years to come. However, during this period, within the world of long-term care, a different reality was developing. Treatment facilities for the mentally ill were not able to receive federal funding, so Medicaid's matching dollars for funding nursing homes became an attractive alternative for these facilities caring for the mentally ill. As a result, more and more nursing homes began opening their doors to mentally ill patients. For the nursing home, it meant increased census and therefore more billable services provided. This shift in the nursing home population brought on new challenges for the nursing home staff, who had little or no training in working with people experiencing mental illness. Screening procedures were eventually put in place to slow this influx of new populations. Even today, many nursing homes remain home to the mentally ill. Keeping the beds full was key to keeping the facility in operation. With that in mind, the administration was often compelled to accept patients other than older adults. In the meantime, staff, not trained to care for the mentally ill, found themselves in dangerous and stressful situations; as a result, many of them moved on to a new facility or left the profession altogether. Again, I am careful to repeat: I know that nursing home administrators are under enormous pressure to produce revenue to keep the facility in operation, yet they are up against a system that dramatically handicaps their efforts.

The federal government, to control costs and improve care, elevated the requirements nursing homes had to meet to qualify for Medicare and Medicaid reimbursements. As a result, the increased requirements meant higher fees to the consumer. In response to this changing environment, a new level of care delivery emerged, assisted living communities. Assisted living communities were less regulated and somewhat easier to fund. As with the nursing home boom during the '60s, assisted living communities during the '80s were popping up everywhere. There are now well over 30,000 assisted living communities in the United States (NCAL, 2016), compared to just over 15,000 nursing homes (AHCA, 2015). Following the introduction of assisted living, the strategy of keeping people at home, or as it is called, "aging in place," emerged. The idea was to bring long-term care into the older adult's home, a place of comfort and familiarity for them. Also, this would move long-term care of older adults away from the institutional medical model towards a more "home-like" social model. As with the nursing home and assisted living booms, home health agencies sprang into being at a breakneck pace. Owners of home health agencies soon discovered, however, that as with nursing homes, they too would face a formidable challenge in maintaining adequate staffing.

The shift away from the medical model to a truly friendlier and more homelike feel was a move in the right direction. In the late '90s, models like the Eden Alternative and Green Houses, developed by Dr. Bill Thomas, offered a potent antidote to the deadly toxins he described as "loneliness, boredom and isolation" (Thomas, 2004).

While the delivery of long-term care continued to evolve, staffing issues remained stubbornly critical and ever increasingly more severe. Vacancies for direct-care workers alone numbered in the hundreds of thousands, which continues to this day as we are approaching nearly a million vacancies. Current projections show that there will be 1.3 million vacancies in long-term care by 2022 (Bureau of Labor Statistics, 2016) So while delivery methods for long-term care may change, the need for qualified and well-trained staff will remain an overwhelming issue.

Average wages for direct-care workers ranged anywhere from $10.05 per hour in Louisiana to $17.93 per hour in Alaska. In Pennsylvania, the average wage for the direct-care worker was $13.68, and in California, the average wage was $14.96. These figures came from the Bureau of Labor Statistics, Occupational Employment Statistics Survey as of May 2015. Imagine a single mother with children working to maintain a household, meeting her needs and the needs of her children at a rate of $10.05 per hour. It didn't happen. Instead, she was likely to take on a second, maybe even a third job, to provide for her family.

As it has been from the beginning, working as a nursing aide was no small task. They arrived at their shift, and they didn't stop moving until their shift ended. Breaks were a rare luxury. The aides were transferring residents, toileting them, giving them showers, changing briefs, feeding them, and then, of course, attending to volumes of charting and paperwork chores. A CNA once told me that when she arrives at her facility, she has twelve hours of work to be done in eight. At the end of her shift, she is exhausted, but she can rest only for a moment until she heads for her second job. With little or no opportunity for pay increases and career advancement, many of them left and continue to leave the nursing home behind to pursue other careers.

After having visited a nursing home in Iowa with some friends, we stopped at a local roadside diner for a late afternoon lunch. The restaurant itself needed a face-lift, a coat of fresh paint would have helped, but more often than not, I've had great meals in places like this, so we pulled over, parked and went inside. The waitress, neatly dressed, and very polite came to greet us. She was wearing an apron and a hair net. She seated us and then she took our order. While we were waiting for our lunch, my friend and I began talking about the staffing situation in nursing homes. We were the only people in the diner at the time. The waitress came to the table with our order, and we started to eat. While we were enjoying the well-prepared meal and continuing our discussion about the nursing home staffing issue, the waitress overheard our conversation. She came over to our table and piped up saying, "I'm a nurse, and I quit." First, I was just shocked, and then I was dismayed. Here was another example of a person who had had enough and quit. I asked her why she quit. Her response revealed what many nursing home workers have faced, "I came to work only to find that I was the only nurse on duty for 100 residents; that's dangerous, and I'm not jeopardizing my license, so I quit, and now I own this diner."

I don't know how many times I've heard stories, not just from RN's, LPN's and nurse aides, but from just about everyone on the nursing home staff, talking about how they not only are working very hard but often lack even the equipment and other resources they need to do their job correctly. While OBRA '87 and the Nursing Home Reform Act did much to regulate the nursing home operation, it did little for the actual work environment.

And continuing today, it's in this chaotic and fluid environment that the Centers for Medicare and Medicaid Systems (CMS) are placing increasing emphasis on nursing staff to provide "person-centered care." One day, as I stood in a wing of a nursing home in Pennsylvania, a facility of several hundred beds, I watched in amazement as two direct-care workers ran from call light to call light, frantically trying to meet the very basic of needs. There was a light above the doorway to each resident's room. One after another, the little white lights were blinking on and off as the residents were hitting their call buttons. One resident needed dressing, another older woman sat on the edge of her bed crying because she needed to go to the bathroom, and yet another resident was roaming the hallway naked. Some of the residents were getting angry and were yelling at the staff.

Meeting the "psycho-social needs of a person" as required by OBRA '87 requires more than meeting basic physical needs. Instead it requires time, time that staff do not have. Volunteers are people who have the time to provide that level of attention. The volunteer is in a perfect position to provide what is now termed, "person-centered" care. Yet, because of OBRA '87 and the subsequent interpretation of those regulations, volunteers were pushed to the sidelines and remain there to the present day. The CMS recognized that when the underlying needs of a person are not met, the nursing home resident may become angry and difficult to manage. Therefore, the requirement to provide person-centered care is correct, but how can already overworked and underpaid staff be expected to provide that level of attention. Sedating people became and continues to be a method for managing people.

Dr. G. Allen Powell discussed this issue at length in his book, *Dementia Beyond Disease* (Power, 2017a). Power (2017a, p. 22) points out that OBRA '87 required and achieved to some degree a reduction in the use of drugs initially developed to treat mental diseases such as schizophrenia. In the course of time, other drugs, "atypical antipsychotic" drugs, were created and presented as causing fewer side effects. In time, care staff turned to these drugs, because they were deemed "safer," for treating persons exhibiting behaviors, or better said, "out-of-character" responses.

The Centers for Medicare and Medicaid through the National Partnership to Improve Dementia Care in Nursing Homes (Centers for Medicare and Medicaid Services, 2016) continued to put pressure on nursing homes to reduce the use of these drugs. According to the CMS report in 2011, 83 percent of the "atypical antipsychotic" drug claims were from nursing home residents having no diagnosis that would indicate the use of these drugs. The CMS set a goal that the use of these drugs was to be reduced by 30 percent by the close of 2016. They reported that as of October 2017 they had met that goal. Is there a resource that can provide personal attention? Yes! The answer lies in training "super" volunteers.

Not only were people being over-medicated, they were not being properly hydrated as well. OBRA '87 took away the volunteer's opportunity to help with the feeding of residents and even providing water for them. The OBRA '87 regulations were interpreted to define feeding and hydrating residents as a nursing duty. Therefore, these tasks now required 75 hours of training at a minimum (training requirement for a nurse aide). Yet, and quite ironically, when family members came to the nursing home to visit their loved one, they were permitted to feed the resident and offer their loved one water, even though they had had no training whatsoever in either of these practices. Once again, a valuable asset, the trained volunteer, who could be trained to provide this support, was pushed to the sidelines.

When I have been in nursing homes during mealtime, I have watched staff serving people their meals. Many of the residents could feed themselves, while still others sat and stared at their plates, some just stirring through the food but not eating. There was little or no conversation at the tables, just a lot of blank stares. And then in a corner area of the dining room reserved for people who could not feed themselves were semi-circular tables, seating about six people, with a nurse-aid seated on a wheeled stool that turned inside the semi-circle where she moved from one end of the semi-circle to the other end. She was feeding the people in an assembly-line fashion, one after the other. Each resident was given a spoonful of something from the plate and then, still seated on her piano-stool, she scooted to the next person. Again, there was little or no conversation, other than prompts from the nurse aide to get the older adult to take a mouthful of food. Some of the residents, when offered the spoon of food, winced and recoiled from the spoon. It was anything but a pleasant experience for the older adult or for the nurse aide, for that matter. At a certain point in this process, the nurse aide or the dietary help cleared away the plates and readied the semi-circular table for the next group of people who needed assistance eating. What should have been a time for pleasant conversation and a relaxing meal had become a frantic and impersonal experience.

Hu, Huang, and Cartwright (1986) found when aides fed residents the experience was about 18 minutes long, as compared to the 99 minutes it took a volunteer or a family member to feed the older adult. The volunteer or the family member not only fed the older adult, but they engaged the older adult in conversation, sharing memories, ideas, making plans and likely sharing a few laughs as well. One experience felt and looked like an assembly line, rushed and impersonal, while the other experience was leisurely, and most importantly, gave the person personal attention. Person-centered care requires the involvement of people who are not in a hurry and who have the time. Person-centered care takes time, valuable time. Time that a volunteer would have.

While talking about urinary tract infections (UTIs) is not a pleasant topic to undertake, it is, however, a serious indicator of the quality of nursing home care the older adult is receiving. Eighteen indicators were chosen by the CMS to reflect the quality of care a nursing home provided. The incident rate of UTIs among nursing home residents is one of those eighteen quality measures specified by federal regulations. Nursing homes are required to report their incident rates for UTIs to the federal government quarterly. These statistics are then used in the rating calculation of nursing homes. The Five-Star Rating System was designed to use the results of UTI reporting combined with the results of the other quality measures. Based on their reported scores, the CMS assigns a star rating to each nursing home. While the causes of UTIs are likely the result of poor proper hygienic care and neglect; i.e., infrequent diaper changes for incontinent residents or the use of urinary catheters, not having enough fluid intake can exacerbate and prolong the infection.

In light of this, the nursing home administrator has a vested interest in keeping the residents of the nursing home hydrated, but, like the challenge of feeding nursing home residents, the challenge of keeping the residents hydrated requires professional staff. However, once again, inadequate staffing levels led to impersonal tactics for providing fluids to the older adult. Direct-care workers responding to endless calls for help or rushing to complete their assigned tasks for the day, have frequently turned to filling a large "sippy cup for the elderly," equipped with a spill-proof lid and a straw or straw-like device, with ice. As the ice melts, the older adult can drink the cold water, that is if they can lift the cup or if they can even reach the cup.

While it is acceptable to give ice chips to certain residents with swallowing problems, more often than not while visiting the nursing home, I've seen every resident's cup or mug filled with ice. I've heard several of the residents complaining that the ice was too cold for them. So rather than having water to drink, the resident was forced to wait for the ice to melt and then come to room temperature before they could drink. Again, because of the current interpretation of OBRA '87 regulations defining the giving of water as a nursing-related task, only professional staff are permitted to offer water.

Couldn't a volunteer be trained to assist with keeping the residents hydrated? Yes, of course they can! And once again, that volunteer has the luxury of time, going from room to room pushing a beverage cart loaded with a variety of juices and water. They would engage the older adult in conversation while offering the older adult something to drink, thus promoting a quicker recovery from the UTI. However, this valuable support for the nursing home resident remains off limits for the volunteer.

Up until 2003, the prevailing interpretation of OBRA '87 prohibited volunteers from assisting the nursing home resident with feeding and drinking fluids because this was a nursing-related duty. In 2003, the CMS recognized that the severe shortage of direct care workers negatively impacted resident quality of care and poor quality of life outcomes. Consequently, the CMS revamped the regulations to include a new nursing home paid position, the "feeding assistant." Nursing home administrators would be permitted to hire part-time workers to receive a minimum of eight hours of training and then be allowed to assist residents during mealtimes. At first, the feeding assistant is limited to residents who need minimal assistance and with time and experience are then moved on to help residents who have more complex needs.

Each state was to be responsible for approving the use of feeding assistants and then be required to develop a training program that met the federal guidelines set forth by the CMS. According to the CMS, there was widespread support for the new position. Wisconsin had already been using feeding assistants for seven years, as had North Dakota. In both cases, the feeding assistant provided welcomed support to the care staff; the feeding assistant was freeing the direct care worker to accomplish more complex tasks or to focus on the residents who had very complex eating needs. What is ironic in all of the discussion and comments received by various individuals and agencies is that the regulation does not require family or volunteers to have the training to feed the resident. The CMS acknowledges that it would be better if family members and volunteers were trained, but that is up to the nursing home administration. The CMS predicted that about 20% of the 15,000 nursing homes would take advantage of the new position, or about 3,400 nursing homes. As of 2004, the National Nursing Home Survey indicated that about 15% of nursing homes were using volunteers for meal assistance (Falkowski, 2013).

The University of Minnesota, Division of Health Policy Management, School of Public Health reported that 21 states had specific content in their regulations for feeding assistants. The point I'm making is that people other than the direct care worker are being trained to provide feeding assistance, to include volunteers.

It can be done, and the Wisconsin feeding assistance program proves that it can be done well.

Again, in the 25 plus years of working in and around the long-term care community, I've witnessed the majority of people working in nursing homes are doing the best they can in a system that burns them out. I'm pretty sure I could count on one hand the number of people I thought were in the wrong job. For example, I witnessed a nurse chastised for working five minutes overtime. She turned to her supervisor and shot back, "What am I supposed to do? Leave the needle hanging in his arm?" One social worker observed, "You can't work here if you care about people." With that, I lay the blame on a system that needs a significant overhaul and is adequately funded.

The topic of abuse is even less attractive than talking about UTIs. It happened well before OBRA '87, and sadly, it continues to this day. The difficulty is that abuse is likely under-reported. Lachs and Pillemer (2015) found that about 10% of nursing home residents, or about 150,000 older adults, experienced some form of abuse. They went on to observe that incident rates are self-reported and likely do not include persons living with dementia, making them even more vulnerable to the abuser. Older adults living in nursing homes have suffered abuse in several ways: neglect, sexual abuse, physical abuse, psychological abuse, and financial abuse. One social worker to whom I spoke relayed how a person experiencing dementia, living in the memory unit of a nursing home, kept complaining that his court-appointed guardian was taking all of his money. At first, because of his dementia, he was not taken seriously. Then, through a series of circumstances, an invoice from his guardian appeared for $250 billing him for a visit the staff knew had never taken place. The guardian was billing the resident's estate for every visit and telephone call, among other services, many of which were never provided.

In the same distasteful vein, a woman was told to lay in her excrement day after day because no one could help her to the restroom. The skin on her backside and legs was covered in sores, some the size of softballs, and the flesh eaten to the bone. Again, this is not the rule, but it's happening. I wondered, if a trained volunteer had been available, could this sort of abuse have been avoided? I could fill a book with the stories I've heard over the years. For this book, I am pointing out that while OBRA '87 raised the bar significantly on nursing home care, it did not solve the staffing problem and it hamstrung the role of the volunteer.

In one case with which I am familiar, a survey team discovered that a nurse aide had a felony charge on her background check. She was immediately fired. This incident led the survey team to review all of the facility's employee records. As a result of the review, eleven nursing home care staff were fired in one week.

In the meantime, while government agencies continue to work to address these issues, couldn't volunteers be on hand to be a second set of eyes or give help to a nurse aide? I firmly believe the answer is "Yes." There are people in our communities looking for meaningful ways to give back. Providing this support would be a meaningful way to make a difference.

There are many ways that trained volunteers could alleviate some of the pressure building inside nursing homes, but the perception of the volunteer as an "amateur" a "non-professional" or *"they're just a volunteer"* was only reinforced by OBRA '87. For certain, going back to the days before OBRA '87 and even further back to the days before any government social programs, elder care was primarily left up to caring citizens, or in other cases, citizens who exploited older adults for momentary gain. With the introduction of government programs, the idea that elder care should be left to the "professionals" took hold. And while this was a good move in many ways, the helpful citizen, the volunteer, was pushed to the background (Kramer, 1981). Smith and Lipsky (1995) observed in their book, *The Politics of Volunteering:*

"... private charity was inconsistent, unreliable, and parochial; thus, the state needed to assume the responsibility for the distribution of services through a state bureaucracy of professional workers who would distribute social welfare services as an entitlement rather than a gift."

With the introduction of Medicare and Medicaid, the emphasis on elder care focused on the elder's physical health. OBRA '87 recognized that the older adult needed more than just medical attention, yet the nursing home administrator, struggling to make ends meet, and struggling to keep adequately staffed, realized that developing a robust volunteer program was not an income producing function of the nursing home. At least, not on the surface. So, while the administrator was required by regulation to have volunteers, the volunteers took a back seat to the nursing home functions that can produce income, i.e., professional nursing staff providing medical services that were billable.

Once again, if you are an administrator of a nursing home, this book is not about chastising you. Instead, my intent is to present an accurate picture of the day-to-day challenges you face running a nursing home and with the goal of convincing you that investing in a robust volunteer program will ultimately have a positive impact on your budget. Chapter Five presents the evidence of the cost-benefit of developing a volunteer program made up of "super" volunteers.

In the end, OBRA '87 laid out a blueprint for providing excellent care of older adults living in nursing homes but in the process, it pushed a valuable resource out of the picture—volunteers. Over the years, nursing homes have used volunteers in a variety of ways, but their engagement in the nursing home was and remains largely guided by the managers of the nursing homes, without a clear and overarching architecture of how volunteers could and should be used in nursing homes. My history and experience in working with volunteers who possess an authentic passion for serving older adults and hearing positive feedback from care staff where those volunteers are now working give me the courage to suggest that volunteers, i.e., "super" volunteers are living in your communities looking for "super" opportunities where they can make a real difference. With that stated, let's move on to the next chapter to discover the meaning of "person-centered" care.

CHAPTER FOUR

We Know Where the Bar Is

———

*"To be human is the need to be loved and to have
someone to love. As far as I can tell, I am still human."*

—CLARENCE AT AGE **92**, LIVING IN A NURSING HOME

N O, I DON'T mean the place where you drink adult bev-
erages, I am referring to the standards of care by which
we measure our efforts. OBRA '87 set the bar for delivering care
for older adults by requiring every nursing home to "provide care
and services in order for each resident to attain or maintain his/
her highest practicable level of physical, mental and psychosocial
well-being." OBRA '87 went a long way in improving the quality
of care for nursing home residents. It hasn't, however, resulted in an
automatic shift from institutional-directed care to person-centered
care. As of this writing, with the Affordable Care Act, person-centered care is mandated and is now a quality indicator for nursing
home care. As a result, there are quite a few discussions about how
to deliver person-centered care. The shift away from the institutional medical model is widely discussed and promoted, yet many
of the 15,000 nursing homes in the United States still strongly
resemble the stereotypical nursing home. Many, if not most, of
these nursing homes struggle to meet just the basic needs of their
residents while simultaneously trying to maintain adequate staffing

levels. In this chapter, I propose that volunteers, properly vetted and trained, have an integral and unique part to play in providing this highly individualized person-centered care. It's within this context that I present this discussion of "person-centered care" and then expand that discussion to include Nolan's Senses Framework (Nolan, Brown, Davies, Nolan, & Keady, 2006) and Dr. Power's discussion of the seven domains of well-being (Power, 2017a).

To begin, let's talk about what "person-centered" care is exactly. Is person-centered care truly person-centered? Tom Kitwood, (1997) a leading pioneer in the field of dementia care, coined the term "person-centered care" and defined personhood as the "standing or status bestowed upon one human being by others in the context of relationship." Kitwood recognized that providing meaningful quality care begins with the realization that one had to fully understand and appreciate the dementia experience from the viewpoint of the patient. It was with this in mind that he developed Dementia Care Mapping, a tool that would allow the observer to evaluate the day-to-day life of the patient experiencing dementia. Dementia Care Mapping is ultimately used to develop a more individualized care plan that would give the staff a sense of confidence that their approach would be tailored to the patient's unique needs. What must be highlighted here is that Kitwood includes the phrase, *"...in the context of relationship,"* in his definition of personhood. To me, this indicates that Kitwood understood that person-centered care could not or would not happen outside of relationships. It is the relationship nurtured between two people that becomes key to understanding the person experiencing dementia as a "person." And so, it is with person-centered care that we approach people, not as a patient held at a professional distance, but rather as a human with whom we are in a relationship, in this instance older adults who need our support. Person-centered care is relational, that is, human beings in relationship with other human beings. We can observe, query, assess, and document our findings in the development of care plans, but ultimately it is the relationship between two people that exposes the real and meaningful needs and cares that produces the quality of life for the nursing home resident. Power suggests that we substitute the word "living" for "care," i.e., person-centered living or relational-living (Power, 2017a). We recognize the frail older adult not as an object to be acted upon but as a human with whom we live in relationship.

Over the years, I've had the opportunity to visit hundreds of nursing homes and visit with dozens of people living and working in nursing homes. During one of my initial visits, I had a conversation with an older woman. She had moved into the nursing home about six months before my visit with her. During our conversation, we talked about her family, her children, her work, and at one point, I asked her what it was like for her now that she was living in a nursing home. She confided in me that she was in a lot of pain. I asked her what sort of pain she was experiencing. Laying her right hand on her heart, she lamented, "I've been here now for about six months, everyone and everything that I knew and loved is now gone. The emotional pain I am feeling is far greater than any physical pain that I feel." At that moment, seeing the sadness in her face and witnessing her disappointment, it became all too clear to me how the painful experience of the debilitating feelings of loneliness and the negative feelings of uselessness can destroy a person's sense of personhood. For this woman, personhood was lost. At this time in her life, there appeared a great and gaping chasm separating her life as she once knew it from what her life had become. "I am alone now with no more reason to live."

For the past 25 years or so, this is a message I frequently hear traveling from nursing home to nursing home. We know from numerous studies that a person's sense of well-being can and does have a significant impact on their physical health, as well as their mental health. Someone experiencing continued feelings of loneliness, helplessness and boredom, the three plagues identified by Dr. Bill Thomas, (1996) face the breakdown and ultimate failure of their immune and endocrine systems. The tearing down process culminates in increased incident rates for chronic illness, depression, dementia, premature death (people just shut down) and most tragic, suicidal ideation and suicide itself.

Until the great recession of 2008, persons 85 years of age and older carried the distinction of being the cohort with the highest incident rate for attempted and successful suicides. Women aged 85 and older had the highest incident rate of attempted suicides, while men 85 years of age and older had the highest rate of successful suicides. Women commonly attempt suicide by overdosing on their medications while men are more likely to use a gun or some other assured method. If women adopted the use of firearms, then women 85 years of age and older would have the highest incident rate of successful suicides. However, with the stock market crash of 2008, persons 45 to 54 moved into first place, with the 85-year old population continuing to follow close behind with regard to suicidal ideation and suicide.

Suicide among older adults is such a sad and truly horrific indictment of our society. Imagine living, learning how to survive and thrive if you will, and finally successfully reaching a good old age of 85, only to come to a point in your life where you believe you are no longer wanted. Now, you languish, cut off from the community and living in a nursing home that strips you of your dignity and your humanity, and treats you as an object. To me, this scenario is more frightening than death itself. Is it any wonder why people living in nursing homes may exhibit negative behavior, become angry, "grumpy," and exhibit out-of-character behaviors?

In the early days of my career, I would perform music in nursing homes. On one such occasion, after I had finished playing for a group of nursing home residents, a nurse aide came into the dining room carrying a small paper cup containing pills and a cup of water. She approached an older woman and handed her the paper cup while instructing her to swallow the pills with the water. Instead, the old woman held the cup up in the air, slightly tilting the cup in my direction so I could see the pills and made this pronouncement: "This is what they think we need. What you are doing is what we need! You make us feel so loved." More than pills, what she and many nursing home residents need is the sense that they are loved, that someone is there just for them as a person worthy of honor and dignity. The person living in the nursing home wants, and I might suggest most people want, to feel that love is freely offered to them without an underlying agenda, a love that is unconditional. The first part of person-centered care is recognizing that the people living in nursing homes have not given up their personhood upon entering the nursing home and that nurturing authentic relationships is paramount to their care.

I can share story after story of how people, experiencing even the most severe degree of dementia, would sing or even dance as I played. One woman sang all three verses of a song and more amazing sang in harmony with me. In another visit, a woman was brought into the dining room to hear my program. At first, she was very disruptive, and the other people complained about her, asking the care staff to please remove her from the room. Once I started to play, the woman became quiet, in fact, after a few minutes I had forgotten that she was in the place. When I finished playing, as was my custom, I went around the room greeting everyone and then one by one they left the room, except for one person, the disruptive woman. I continued packing up my gear, and finally, it was time for me to leave. The room now was empty except for this one woman who sat motionless before me. My curiosity got the best of me, so I approached her. Her head was bowed, and her hands were folded and resting on the table. I asked her if she was feeling better. In an entirely coherent response, she looked up into my face, making eye-contact and said, "Yes. You know, Jesus loves me this I know. That might be the only thing worth remembering." With my jaw gaping, I stood in front of her, stunned.

Once I pulled myself together, I agreed with her saying that she might be right and then I said good-bye. As I left, she was still sitting there, quietly in a posture of what appeared to be one of prayer. In this way, and at this early point in my career, I believe I unwittingly participated in and experienced the power of person-centered care. By luck, I happened to play a song that evoked her response and gave her some relief from her predicament. Today, I would prefer not to rely on luck; it would be better for me to spend time with someone, to get to know them, to discover their history, their likes, their dislikes and the things that bring meaning to them. Nurturing that relationship, I could, with knowledge, not luck, play a song that would be meaningful to them. Knowing what I know now, just by chance, I may have helped that woman avoid a dose of an antipsychotic drug to calm her.

Antipsychotic and hypnotic drugs have been used for many years to manage "difficult" people. There are rare times when the use of these drugs might be appropriate, (with a strong emphasis on the word "rare"), but all too often they are the remedy of the first choice rather than the last. The use of antipsychotics and similar drugs have no place in the person-centered mandate. Many times, the staff sedate older adults for acting out or being unmanageable, when all the while the older adult wants, is seeking, needs, and hopes for, is to be treated as a person, as a human being with unique needs and desires. Not taking the time or not having the time, as the case is for many care staff, to discover, to address and to meet those unmet underlying needs, often results in negative behaviors or more accurately identified as out-of-character responses. The term "negative behavior" infers that a person is acting with malice and fully aware of their actions, whereas "out-of-character response" describes behavior that, under normal conditions, they would not have displayed in such a manner. The challenge to care staff is to discover the older adult's underlying need(s) and to determine how to satisfy those needs. Simply medicating people for out-of-character responses is treating a symptom of an underlying cause while only providing an unsatisfactory and temporary solution. This topic is well discussed at length by Dr. Allen Power in his book: *Dementia Beyond Drugs: Changing the Culture of Care,* (Power, 2017b). Taking the time to befriend the resident to get to know them, their history, while consulting with family members to add to that cache of information, takes time, but the solutions developed from that information are lasting, if not permanent, and certainly not as severe as administering drugs. Person-centered care recognizes personhood and that person-centered care requires time.

Dr. Power tells the story of an older man who was living in a nursing home. Because of his dementia, he was moved to the "memory" unit. The term "memory unit" is a topic for another day. As the story goes, every morning about 6 am, the older man would walk to a door in the memory unit that opened onto a fenced-in courtyard. While looking through the glass door, he would rattle the push bar on the door trying to open it. When the door would not open, he became agitated shaking the door even more violently. The care staff attempted to pull him away from the door, but he became even more belligerent with the care staff. Finally, they sedated him. This event took place every morning for the first week of his stay. Frustrated, the nursing home staff contacted the old man's family asking for their help. One of the family members realized what the older man was trying to do. She explained to the nurse, every morning the first thing her father would do would be to go into the farmyard to check on his livestock. When he was satisfied that all was well with them, he would return to the house and have breakfast. Armed with that information, the next morning at the nursing home the staff waited for the older man to come to the door, this time however the door was unlocked. Like clockwork, he came to the door, pushed on it and went outside. The staff watched him as he went out, stood in the courtyard for a few minutes and then turning back, he returned to the nursing home. There was no fighting, no angry outbursts, no agitation, just an old man who had the satisfaction of checking to make sure his cows were okay.

Consider how simple this solution is. Volunteers properly trained have the time to do this kind of research and can be your window to discovering the underlying needs of a resident, rather than learning that care staff had to wrestle and fight with an older man only to then sedate him.

I attend national conferences when I'm able. During one breakout session whose topic of discussion was person-centered care, the presenters developed an assessment tool consisting of several dozens of questions for determining the personal preferences of newly admitted nursing home residents. What became apparent to me at that point was that this version of person-centered care was an extension of the medical model. As Daniella Greenwood, Strategy and Innovation Manager, Arcare, Melbourne, Australia said to me during one of our conversations, "…it's bossing you around in a very individualized way." (D. Greenwood, personal communication, November 6, 2016). While this sort of device may provide a starting point for the staff, person-centered care is more than developing a list of the resident's preferences. Person-centered care means, or should mean, cultivating close and caring relationships with the residents. Person-centered care is not about seeing this is the "person I care for" but rather, seeing "this person is my friend. We have become friends."

Person-centered care encourages the care staff to engage in meaningful conversations that lead to insight about the people for whom they care. "Tell me something about yourself." "What would you like to wear today?" "What are your favorite colors?" "At what time do you like to eat breakfast and what do you like to eat for breakfast?" "What are your favorite meals?" "In what sort of activities do you like to participate?" "What are your hopes?" "What are your dreams?" Listening carefully to the resident's responses and offering meaningful and thoughtful feedback to the resident lays the groundwork for creating the intimacy between the caregiver and the care receiver required to create authentic person-centered care. The perception that "…someone cares about me…" is very powerful, both for the caregiver and the care receiver. However, the brutal reality of the nursing home environment is that care staff most likely do not have the flexibility or time, even if they have the will, to offer this kind of personalized attention. An authentic relationship requires an intimacy developed over time.

In discussing relationship building, we come to the construct of intimacy; for some, that can be a frightening proposition. Intimacy takes the relationship and moves it from a casual meeting to an engagement where we know the intimate details of a person's life. Years ago, I retrieved an article by Dr. Kalman Heller, "It's Fear of Intimacy, Not Lack of Time" (2000). In the article, he posits the idea that we are afraid of getting too close to someone. We fear possible rejection and disappointment if we show our true colors. So rather than pursue close relationships, we choose the path of excusing ourselves by hiding behind our "busy-ness." "I'd love to stop and spend some time getting to know you, but I just don't have the time right now to do that, maybe we can get together next week." Of course, when next week arrives, there's a new set of "reasons" why we cannot pursue the relationship. Dr. Heller goes on to discuss that opening oneself to someone else is a "risky business… requiring a serious commitment to the relationship." It requires sharing our inner thoughts and fears and facing the reality that we might face rejection; at that point, we find ourselves in a precarious "dance." When we feel ourselves getting too close to someone, we back away, thereby creating this oscillation between closeness and distance. Why is this important to the topic of person-centered care? Because we all need this sense of intimacy, and when it is missing from our lives, from the lives of the people for whom we care, what are the outcomes?

Person-centered care requires intimacy that goes well beyond meeting just the basic needs of the residents and certainly well beyond a simple assessment tool. Person-centered care is much more than just making sure that the older adult has had their medications, their nutritional needs met, that they are hydrated, properly turned, toileted and bathed, that they are getting to sleep in or skip breakfast or have pizza for lunch. Person-centered care goes well beyond making sure that the older adult is receiving proper care and recreation. Person-centered care necessarily includes making sure that the older adult feels loved, accepted, and cherished. This brand of care goes beyond just meeting the physical needs of the person. It requires a conscious and intentional effort on the part of the caregiver to create a bond, a relationship, a partnership that incorporates the older adult's emotional and psychological needs while taking what is being communicated by the older adult seriously. The caregiver will listen to the older adult with understanding and intent to act upon what the older adult has expressed.

Person-centered care is stopping to be "in the moment," to be "present," to focus, to listen and to learn from the people for whom we care. Person-centered care represents becoming the friend who gives the older adult a sense of control over their care. "The aim is customization of care, according to individual needs, desires, and circumstances. It also implies transparency, with a high level of accountability of the care system to the patient," (Berwick, 2002). Without "person-centered" care there really is *no* care. Daniella Greenwood, (D. Greenwood, personal communication, November 6, 2016) describes it this way: "The idea of being old and vulnerable equates to being sick, is a problem. Old people are vulnerable, and they need critical support and assistance, but that's one small part of what they need, the rest of it is called life."

Person-centered care provides *"life."*

"I have a lot of people around me, nurses, nurse aides, but there is no one here just for me." These words, spoken to me by an older woman living in a nursing home, revealed her need for more than just physical cares and recreation. She was expressing the need for love and intimacy, the need to have a confidant, the need for someone who knows *"me"* personally, someone who will talk "with" me not "to" or "at" me. In an interview I conducted with Emile Strommen Olsen, senior program designer for DesignIt, and her client Stephanie Helland, the administrator for Kristiansund kommune in Norway, Emilie described the process for creating and implementing the volunteer program for this community. As part of the design process, the designers asked residents what they wanted from this volunteer program. The resident's responded saying: "We just want one person to talk to and do "normal" stuff, not big activities where everyone participates at once," (E. Olsen, personal communication, February 23, 2016).

Halfway around the world, Daniella Greenwood, in talking with her residents, discovered this same desire for *"normal."* Daniella talked about how she kept hearing about these *"fantastic"* relationships that the residents had with the cleaning staff. So, she asked them, "What is it about these relationships?" And their response was, "It's just a 'normal' relationship." At that point, Daniella says she had an epiphany moment realizing that the cleaning people were probably one of the few people that came into the resident's room without an agenda to do something to them, i.e., bathe them, toilet them or dress them, etc.

Here again, "super" volunteers, that is volunteers properly vetted and trained, can be invaluable. They too, come into the relationship with the residents without an agenda. The "super" volunteer can provide that sense of *"normal."*

The quote that I opened this chapter with, from 92-year old Clarence, reveals this need does not go away. Clarence declared, "To be human is the need to be loved and to have someone to love. As far as I can tell, I am still human." As we age, our need to be in an intimate relationship only intensifies and when that need goes unmet, we become empty shells of what we once were. We may become lethargic and may even resign ourselves to accepting impersonal poor care (Simmons & Rahman, 2014) a form of self-neglect. Person-centered care is knowing each older adult living in a nursing home as a "…whole person" (Van Haitsma et al., 2014).

Nolan et al., (1997, 2006) took a different perspective on the attempt to provide person-centered care and developed an approach he called the Senses Framework, a relationship-centered approach. It shouldn't come as a surprise to you by this point in the chapter that I prefer this terminology for it is the quality of the relationship between the caregiver and the care receiver that is at the heart of person-centered care. Nolan recognized that quality of care and quality of life were not the same thing; quality of care is inextricably tied to the relationships between practitioners and older adults, practitioners and the older adult's family, practitioners with the community, and finally practitioners with other practitioners. The perception of quality of life is subjective and requires that each person who is receiving care have a key input as to what quality of life means to them. The resident's perception of quality of life becomes the foundation for how care is given. The word Sense was chosen deliberately by Nolan to indicate the subjectivity of quality of life and quality of care.

Nolan also recognized that the perception of older adults having little or no value in society impacts the perception staff hold concerning their work. If the older adult is no longer important to society, if they have no relevance, no meaning, then this job of caring for older adults must also be unimportant and irrelevant to society. Furthermore, the job has no real meaning. I learned this early on, even in the world of volunteerism, that when I decided to serve people who were marginalized by society, I became marginalized as well. Therefore, the Senses Framework applied not only to the person receiving care, but it also applied to the person giving care. With that in mind, the Sense Framework represented a complete approach to providing person-centered care, which focused only the care receiver.

It is clear that older adults want "…a normal relationship," and that care staff want to feel that their work matters. The six senses that Nolan (1997, 2006) presented are: security, continuity, belonging, purpose, fulfillment, and significance. Each sense carries a description that is unique for each actor: the older adult, the care staff, and the family. For each player, there is a description of what that "sense" means to them. In each case, the parties want to have a "sense" they are free from threat or censure. The older adult's biography looks to their past for continuity to provide context for the present, while the care staff is looking for continuity through a good work experience that extends from the beginning of their career to the present. Each group wants to feel that they belong to a community made up of meaningful relationships. These groups want the opportunity to set and reach goals, i.e., affording them a sense of purpose. Each group member wants to take satisfaction in their accomplishments and feel valued as a person that matters.

These six senses apply to the volunteer as well, for they too are a stakeholder in the sphere of the nursing home resident.

From the vantage point of relationship-centered caring, our understanding of autonomy moves away from the perspective of an individual surviving on their own, to one of an individual immersed in a complex network of "…social relationships," that provide needed support. The "super" volunteer is a critical participant in that support network for they have the time and the training to provide that level of care.

So, can nursing home staff provide person-centered care that is, in fact, more accurately described as relation-centered care? The short answer is, "Yes, but it is not easy." During our conversation, Daniella relayed a story that offered insight about how nursing staff may struggle with the concept of seeing the older adult, not as a patient but as a friend. Recognizing that relationship was integral to providing quality care, Daniella approached the staff about this. She was met with a great deal of resistance, which she interpreted as the staff being mean-spirited. One day, and at a point where Daniella felt that she might resign, she overheard a conversation between a mother and her two children. Daniella was out of sight from the conversation, so she could not see who was speaking. Daniella said the conversation was *"gorgeous"* as she heard a mother talking to her two children, lifting their spirits and raising their self-esteem. The children had had a bad day at school. "I poked my head around the corner to see who it was and there was one of those care staff that I thought was so mean with all these skills." It was at that moment Daniella realized that the staff already had the skills to provide person-centered care, but what they needed was permission to use those skills while caring for their residents. Care staff is often taught to keep a professional distance, as their patients particularly in acute care settings are with them for a short period. In the long-term care setting, this mindset does not make sense, according to Daniella, as many of the nursing home residents may be with the staff for years. The staff want the people for whom they are caring to feel whole, well, happy, and loved. In this case, they just needed permission to do so. A full description of Daniella's work at Arcare appears in Chapter Seven.

For many, the care staff are frustrated as they continually face short-staffing, low wages, and exhaustion from working several jobs to make ends meet. In many cases, the care staff operate in a burned-out state of mind, making it difficult if not impossible, for them to offer this intimate level of care and attention. Until we correct those issues, person-centered care will remain a desirable, noble, worthwhile, but elusive goal. One staff member confided in me that after working in a nursing home for several months, "You cannot care about people and work here." Soon after that conversation with her, I learned she had quit working at the nursing home. How many great and caring people like this person become disillusioned and ultimately leave the workforce? I would suggest that number is much more significant than we know.

But…yes, nursing home staff can be trained to provide person-centered care to the extent that time will allow. There is exploration of some excellent programs and other strategies to change this dynamic. For example, permanently assigning staff to residents is one strategy. Staff, not rotating assignments, will provide care for the same people day in and day out. This strategy helps the staff person get to know the people for whom they care on a personal level, learn the nuances of their residents' needs, and become their friend. Burgio, Fisher, Fairchild, Scilley, and Hardin (2004) found that staff permanently assigned to residents reported higher job satisfaction and that residents were sad to see their caregivers leave at the end of the day. Caregivers formed bonds with the people under their care, as a result. However, the study also reported that absenteeism and burnout were not impacted as permanent assignments did not solve the issues often associated with a chaotic and time-crunched environment.

So much of our identity, that is, "who we perceive ourselves to be and what we like to do" is wrapped in the kinds of food we like to eat and how we like to prepare that food. With that in mind, mealtime, what should be an opportunity to foster person-centered care and intimate relationships, becomes a frantic race to the finish. The preparation and the presentation of the food, especially if it has been pureed, can be objectionable and unappealing to the resident. A very good friend of my family, who lived to be 106 years old, detested the food served in the nursing home. On getting her meal, she would stare down at her plate and begin to stir the food around, attempting to make it look like she had eaten some of it.

The staff got wise to her, and this resulted in the doctor's order to have her moved to the section of the dining room for people who needed assistance with eating. We knew that she was quite content with her Ensure and her coffee with cream and sugar, and at the age of 106, why not! We also came to know the aides that cared for her reasonably well and told them that the old woman was quite content with her current diet, but it was to no avail. The doctor's order came in on Friday for our friend to be moved to the feeding table. We didn't know this happened until the following Monday morning when the two aides who we had befriended ran into our office weeping, reporting to us that our friend had been forced fed, aspirated and was now in the hospital. I stayed with my friend, a true matriarch, by her hospital bedside until she died several days later. She was a beautiful woman with a wonderful history, having lived so well, only to die in this fashion. It was a tragic ending for her and the result of a total lack of understanding of person-centered care.

Certified Nursing Assistants (CNAs) are trained to provide feeding assistance, but again, time becomes an issue. The Vanderbilt Paid Feeding Assistant Training, developed by the Vanderbilt Center for Quality Aging, is one example of a training program for feeding residents that opens the door for persons other than CNAs to provide feeding assistance, such as other nursing home staff, family members, and volunteers. This expansion allows trained individuals to feed people and free CNAs to provide assistance to people with very complex feeding issues. The training program transforms mealtime from a "hurry up and eat" environment to a social event, a gathering of friends filled with conversation and relationship building. Similarly, "Dining with Friends," developed by the Alzheimer's Resource Center of Connecticut, Inc., provides strategies and tactics to make mealtime enjoyable by making sure the food being served is pleasing to the eye. Even pureed food is reconstituted to appear as it did in its original form. Pureed pizza is reshaped to look like slices of pizza! Dining music is included as well as offering the residents "dining scarves" rather than bibs to avoid the inference that people are babies again who need to wear bibs while being fed. As with the Vanderbilt Paid Feeding Assistant Training, "Dining with Friends" returns mealtime to a social gathering, engaging both the person assisting the resident as well as the person needing feeding assistance in a pleasing and relaxed relationship.

Yes, providing person-centered care is possible, but it is not easy when the caregiver is running from one end of their shift to the other trying to meet the basic human needs of the residents. Without a doubt, we must continue to encourage and train professional care staff about what it means to provide person-centered care and how to provide that level of care. However, as long as the staffing issues continue to exist, i.e., inadequate staffing ratios, substandard wages, high turnover and so on, to what degree can we realistically expect care staff to provide person-centered care?

As I have already observed, person-centered care requires the professional care staff to take time to listen to the people for whom they care and to be responsive to an older adult's expressed needs and desires. Studies have shown that, at best, this is a genuine challenge in the chaotic and fluid environment of the nursing home. Simmons et al.,(2014) observed staff over 12 weeks, to discover that only 8% of the residents were being given choices as to when and where to eat breakfast and 21% had choices for when to get out of bed in the morning. Van Haitsma et al., (2014) stated nursing homes reported that inadequate staff time (55%), staff resistance (44%), and staff turnover (11%) are serious challenges to implementing person-centered care. It should be noted that most of the homes in her evaluation were four-and-five-star communities. What happens to person-centered care in poorer performing nursing homes? It is more likely that they will focus on providing basic care, rather than person-centered care (Van Haitsma et al., 2014). Does this mean it is impossible for the nursing home staff to provide person-centered care? No. As I mentioned previously, there are notable efforts and training to train the care staff about person-centered care. While CNAs and paid staff can be and are trained in these techniques, "super" volunteers can undoubtedly be taught to perform them, as well.

There is another dynamic in play that I need to highlight here. Bangerter, Van Haitsma, Heid, and Abbott (2015) revealed a resident's attitude about care staff that caught my attention. While the resident expects and desires a friendly and respectful staff person to care for them, one who is willing to "really" listen to them, what the resident wants more from the care staff is a "professional" who knows what they are doing. One of the residents of the study put it this way: "'They are here to do a job. Not to like me or care about me. I don't look at it like we have a bond or friendship.'"

In reading this for the first time, it struck me that the attempt of offering "person-centered care" may be hindered in one important aspect: the staff member will be coming to the resident with an agenda, i.e., "I've got to get this task done. There is something I need to do to you, or I need to have you do." Regardless of how well the staff member is addressing the older adult's needs, the older adult may feel that the relationship is contrived or forced. The staff person comes not just to have a friendly chat, but to complete tasks dictated by lists of needs to be completed in a specified timeframe. The resident senses this, even though the staff are trying to offer friendly conversation. This leads me to believe that person-centered care, or to use the term relational care, is more than just friendly conversation.

Conversely, the volunteer trained to provide person-centered attention is coming to the resident without that overarching "task to be completed" feeling. In thinking about this further, it seems that person-centered care requires the presence of this unfettered relationship with a volunteer. These relationships form without strings attached or coached behaviors from either party, volunteer or resident. I've been asked by nursing home residents on several occasions: "Why are you here?" I think the underlying message in this question is, "I know what this place is, and I know that you could be anywhere in the world right now. Why did you choose to come here to be with me?" And if I can add, "What is your agenda?" The men living in a veteran's home were laying bets that I was either a seminarian or doing community service time. No one could believe I just wanted to be there with them. When they realized I had no real agenda other than to spend time with them, they opened up to me creating a relationship with no strings attached. This discussion leads me to ask, "Is the 'super' volunteer an indispensable element of person-centered care?" Yes, and yes! As I alluded to above, to administrators, the relationship your residents have with the staff will be of a different brand than the relationships your residents will have with your "super" volunteers. Just as a reminder, your "super" volunteers have gone through a stringent vetting and training process demonstrating to you a high level of commitment and passion for serving in your community. The "super" volunteer truly cares and wants to create authentic relationships with the residents. When I asked Jill Woodward, administrator of the Elizabeth Knox Hospital and Home, how she put together such a great volunteer program her immediate response was, "We started by hiring a great volunteer coordinator." (personal communication, August 30, 2016). Great volunteers need great leadership to thrive and to grow in their roles. I will discuss Jill's program in detail in Chapter Seven.

One of the beautiful qualities of the "super" volunteer is empathy. They have been trained to listen, listen, and listen some more. They know how to key in on recurring themes from those conversations. They have the "luxury of time" (Gross, 1961). Because they are not on the payroll, (again, I'm not replacing paid staff with free labor), they can spend as much time as needed getting to know someone. Using their reflective listening skills, they can get the resident to open up and talk freely about their desires, their needs, and their dreams. The "super" volunteer has the sensitivity to make mental notes about recurring themes such as: "I miss my home or my spouse," "My family is important to me," "I feel so alone and useless," and a myriad of other thoughts. The resident may be reticent to open up to the care staff out of fear of reprisal, whether real or imagined; perhaps the quality of the relationship does not encourage that sort of openness. Many times, during my visits, residents have asked me to not divulge to staff what they have confided in me. I honor that request as not to threaten our relationship in which trust has become a key ingredient. Mistrust of the care staff may add a barrier to developing this brand of a meaningful relationship.

One of my many great experiences took place while visiting an older woman, a retired concert pianist. She commented to me that it had been such a long time since she had heard Claude Debussy's *La Mer,* which means *The Sea.* It is a beautiful symphonic work with which I was familiar because of my musical training. Later that day, the thought occurred to me to surprise her by bringing my recording of this musical work to her on my next visit to listen to it together. On my next visit, I brought the recording with me and presented it to her. She was more than ecstatic, and together we let the music carry us away to some distant place far beyond the nursing home. When it ended, through her tears she thanked me profusely. Knowing what I know now about the impact of person-centered care and music, I wondered and marveled about the impact that had on her. I know that I began receiving letters from various parts of the country written by members of her family and thanking me for doing this thing for their mother. I believe she had written letters to just about every living relative telling them about this person who did this thing for her. For me, I could hardly believe her reaction. At the time, I was still naïve and did not realize what I had done for her. Now looking back, I'm glad I made that decision, even not knowing how profound an impact it would have on her. Maybe it was better, I did not know. Here was a need that a large group activity likely could not have met, that the staff might have struggled to meet, but a volunteer with a personal relationship with the resident could easily meet. Together, this woman and I had the opportunity to do something "normal." We talked about that day for many visits to come.

This morning I awoke at 5:00 a. m., sipped a cup of coffee, put on my sweats and headed for the gym. I mounted the elliptical machine and for the next forty minutes practiced interval training, i.e., 90 seconds of moderate pace alternating with 30 seconds of an all-out sprint. From there I headed back home to eat breakfast and view the news feeds on my tablet. It was a "normal" start to my day. If asked by a researcher how satisfied am I with my life, I would likely respond, "For the most part I am satisfied, but there are a few areas for improvement." This response is what I believe most people would give. Self-perception of one's sense of well-being, of course, is quite subjective. If you were to ask a nursing home resident the same question the response might be something along the same lines. It's fascinating and interesting to hear these sorts, of responses from people who are likely living in an environment that deprives them of "normal" living. Power (2017a) in his search for finding the "pathway" to well-being presents seven domains of well-being that nullifies the stigma that people living in nursing homes cannot have quality of life, cannot experience growth, and can no longer learn or experience joy. By addressing those seven domains: identity (preserving the sense of self); growth (having opportunities to learn new things); autonomy (having the freedom to choose); security (freedom from fear); connectedness (feeling engaged); meaning (experiencing hope even in the face of difficult situations) and joy (overall satisfaction with life as it is) we move away from the biomedical model of care towards a more holistic approach which recognizes people having their medical needs met is only a tiny part of true "person-centered" care. These seven domains are not limited to the nursing home resident but apply to all participants to include staff, family and yes, the volunteer.

With that in mind, creating "authentic partnerships" (DuPuis et al., 2012) and agreeing with Dr. Power that this is likely the best way to describe the relationships between all of the players and should be the goal of all involved, isn't this what we all desire in our relationships with other people? Don't we immediately sense whether a person is approaching us with a sincere desire to know us, to be with us, to be there for us or are they coming to us to gain some advantage for themselves, i.e., a selfish purpose. Of course, we do.

"Super" volunteers are in a perfect position to provide that level of care. They are sincere, compassionate and passionate about serving older adults. They bring with them the innate desire to create these authentic partnerships, not for personal gain but to be, as Mother Teresa once said, "...to be somebody to someone." Imagine a nursing home full of these "super" volunteers creating these relationships, not only with residents, but with the staff as well. The well-trained "super" volunteer understands these concepts, bringing meaning and life to residents and validation to the staff.

In my dissertation, using the National Nursing Home Survey 2004, I showed empirically a positive and direct relationship between individualized activities between volunteers and residents producing positive results in quality measures represented by the proxy variable of nursing hours per patient day. While the results can be argued, it is clear that nursing home residents who are engaged in "authentic partnerships" have fewer falls, less frequent urinary tract infections, require less medication, and express a higher level of well-being. The care staff experiences fewer interruptions and experiences the same uplift as the residents as they watch the "super" volunteer interacting with their residents. But seeing volunteers in this critical role, allowing for the expansion of their role in the long-term care environment requires a paradigm shift, a shift that can only be brought about by visionary leadership willing to change the system.

In the current staffing environment, we must not hesitate to take advantage of every resource available to us. This includes creating the "super" volunteer, someone who has withstood a stringent vetting process and completed intensive training. Through this onboarding process, they have the opportunity to demonstrate their passion and commitment for caring and wanting to make a real difference. This "super" volunteer has the luxury of time, the flexibility to pause and take the time to learn a person's history, their desires, their likes and dislikes, their hopes and their dreams. As early as 1961, Ann Gross (Gross, 1961) recognized this and advocated for this level of volunteer activity in nursing homes. Volunteers have the "luxury of time" according to Gross (1961 p. 101). And isn't time the real issue? As for volunteers filling the need for person-centered, relational-care, some barriers prevent them from doing more.

To begin, volunteer programs are non-income producing functions. Volunteers are required by regulation, but the program does not generate income. The nursing home cannot bill for volunteer services; therefore, the volunteer programs take a back seat to "billable" services. And I do not fault administrators for this; many of them struggle to keep their doors open, let alone invest heavily in a volunteer program whose return on investment may be difficult to measure. However, when the residents feel loved, safe and connected, and the staff feels validated by the community for the work they do, the impact on turnover and retention rates, the use of antipsychotics and the overall quality of care leading to improved quality of life, are significant. The quality of care improves quality of life not only for the people living in the nursing home but for the people working in the nursing home.

Yes, we know where the bar is, but we need to be willing to innovate, train and condition ourselves to jump that high. It should be clear by now that the "super" volunteer is an indispensable part of the long-term care environment.

CHAPTER FIVE

The Five Excuses Why We Can't Do This

"The only thing standing between you and your goal is the *!#% story you keep telling yourself as to why you can't achieve it."

—JORDON BELFORT

WHEN PRESENTING MY case for expanding the role of volunteers in nursing homes, I'm invariably met with a barrage of comments indicating that, despite some knowledge about the issues, people's awareness is very narrow. Now, before you close the book, hear me out. Through my experience in developing training programs and training volunteers for nursing homes, it has become abundantly clear to me (and to others for that matter) that there are people living in our communities who are willing and capable of making the extraordinary effort to learn new skills and to make strong commitments to serving as volunteers in their local nursing home. In this chapter, I am going to identify five common barriers that seem to hinder nursing home leadership from pursuing a meaningful, well-designed, well-coordinated volunteer program. I hope this information will undo the negative perceptions about volunteers taking on expanded roles in the nursing home. I hope I can help you see that instituting a robust volunteer program will be good for improving quality of care and ultimately the quality of life for the people living in nursing homes. In addition, a volunteer program will also have a positive impact on job satisfaction among your staff and upon your image in your community. We who work in the world of volunteers bring this confusion on ourselves for not insisting that only high-quality, professionally trained volunteer coordinators are permitted to oversee the nursing home volunteer program.

When you are hiring a director of nursing, what qualifications do you require? What level of nursing experience do you expect? Do you believe that putting only qualified care staff in charge is imperative? Of course, you do!

Your volunteers should get the same scrutiny as your care staff. They should meet the standards you have set for your paid staff. Am I putting the director of volunteers on par with the director of nursing? Absolutely! The director of nursing should have a nursing degree, with years of proven experience working in the long-term care setting and so on. The same should be true for the person you put in charge of your volunteer program. She/he should have formal and documented training in volunteer management with a proven track record of successfully managing volunteers. The paradigm shift here is, the person you choose to develop and manage your volunteer program should have the education and experience that qualifies them as a professional director of volunteer involvement (Ellis, 2010). This takes your program from being shoddy and unreliable to be an excellent and valuable component in the delivery of care.

What seems to be more common is the "necessary but not very important chore" of developing a volunteer program falls to the activities director, or the life enrichment coordinator or someone else on your staff who is "volunteered" to take on the task. The task becomes a side-line job. Statistically, it is unlikely the staff in those positions have had any necessary training, and more critically, they may not have adequate time for developing a quality and sustainable program. Managing the volunteer program is, and should be recognized as, a full-time job to be led by a trained professional, just as you would any other member of your management staff. If that doesn't happen, then the program will most likely falter at best, and may even collapse, leading the managers, the directors, and staff to conclude that volunteer programs do not work. Well, if you don't put the right fuel in your car, it won't work either.

If you make a serious investment in your volunteer program, it will reap serious rewards; rather than being an unstable and stumbling program, it will evolve into a self-sustaining resource that not only enriches the lives of the people for whom you provide care, but also will bring a sense of satisfaction to your professional care staff. The professional care staff, i.e., nurses and certified nursing assistants (CNAs) with whom I've spoken tell me that observing a volunteer spending time with one of their residents in one-on-one visits and personal activities, such as letter reading and/or writing, brings them a sense of satisfaction. The staff members know "their patients" are getting what they really need. The professional caregiver experiences a lift in their spirit that translates into job satisfaction. They feel the joy that the older adult feels. They say that seeing the volunteer giving that personalized attention to someone gives them a sense of comfort and a sense of positive well-being, knowing that what the volunteer is doing is what their residents need.

Residents can tell us what they need if we give them the opportunity and time to express their needs, their desires and what matters to them most. Professional directors of volunteers can develop training programs to match the needs of your long-term care community. Volunteers, adequately vetted and trained, can then become your eyes and ears. Volunteers have the "luxury of time"

(Gross, 1961) and the opportunity to learn what really matters to each older adult. I think I've said this several times in this book, but it bears repeating: So many times, residents' behaviors are not appropriately treated because the staff does not have the time to discover the residents' underlying needs. Instead, the symptom(s) of the need is managed rather than meeting the need. Time is on the side of the volunteer! Train them and let them discover what matters the most to people.

So, what are the five excuses for not pursuing a robust volunteer program? They are:

1. volunteers create problems and lead to liability issues,

2. volunteer programs are unsustainable because volunteers are unreliable,

3. volunteers will replace paid employees,

4. policy prohibits volunteers from taking on expanded roles in the care of the residents as well as the staff,

5. volunteer programs are expensive and in the end produce very little output for all the money that is spent on them.

Over the next few pages, I am going to help you see that all five of these perceptions or "excuses" are simply challenges that can be turned into opportunities for creating a great volunteer program. In this chapter, I address each one; in Chapter Seven, I present descriptions of several long-term care communities who have made serious investments in their volunteer programs, along with the outcomes that each of these programs has produced. So, to begin let's address the question that I am asked immediately when I present this concept, "What about liability?"

"What about liability?"

Whenever I present the concept of expanding the role of volunteers in nursing homes, one of the first things people ask me is "What about liability?" I echo back to them, "What about it?" I'll admit that the liability issue is a difficult one, but it's not a new issue and should not keep you from pursuing your desire to build a robust volunteer program. How do you address liability now with your employees? Why would your approach to liability change for volunteers? Susan Ellis (2010), founder and president of Energize, Inc. deals with the issue of liability very well in her book *From the Top Down*. She writes, and I agree, that volunteers are no more prone to accidents and mishaps than any of your employees. I want to take it a step further and suggest that volunteers may be less prone to risk because they come to you because they "want to make a difference." Volunteers come to you, not because they needed a job, but because they are looking for opportunities where they can make a meaningful contribution. They want to give back to their community in a meaningful way. They have a passion for working with older adults, and now your nursing home presents them with such an opportunity to fulfill their desire. I would suggest that the person who makes that level of commitment, out of altruistic motivations, then correctly vetted, trained and managed, will likely be even more conscientious than paid staff.

To continue, Ellis (2010, p. 188) recommends that, ahead of time, you identify potential threats and situations that could create risks involving volunteers. With those items identified, develop a list of "do's and don'ts," protocols for volunteers to follow in those identified circumstances and document that the volunteer understands and agrees to comply with your clearly stated expectations. For example, what should a volunteer do when a resident is calling for the volunteer to transfer that resident from her wheelchair to the toilet? What should the volunteer do in that situation? What should a volunteer do if a resident begins to fall? What should a volunteer do if they see someone aspirating while trying to eat? These are just a few of many possible scenarios that a volunteer could experience. In fact, in the Centers for Medicare and Medicaid Services (CMS) regulations, volunteer training must include a variety of circumstances to include emergency management, infection control, elder abuse and so on. A series of these scenarios should be included in your initial volunteer training and again, just as you would with a new employee, document the training. If the volunteer violates the rules, do what you do with any employee, you fire them! When you set the bar high, you find and interact with people who can jump that high. And you will have a waiting list of people wanting to volunteer. I'll talk about that in Chapter Seven.

Our training at Community 360° included a "content review" assessment at the conclusion of the training. This assessment requires the volunteer to respond to a series of questions based on the content of the training. The trainer reviews their responses and the assessment is then signed and dated by the volunteer. It then becomes part of their permanent file.

In addition to identifying potential risks, make sure your insurance policy covers your volunteers. Again, I would recommend you sit down with your agent and risk assessment manager to discuss potential risks so that you will cover all contingencies. You go through this process when dealing with your paid employees, now you are adding another group, but these are not "walk-in" volunteers, these are the volunteers who have been thoroughly screened, thoroughly vetted, and well trained. They are your "super" volunteers.

Finally, in addressing liability there are federal and state "Good Samaritan" laws in place to protect the activities of volunteers; there is the Volunteer Protection Act of 1997 (105th Congress of the United States, 1997). While this law does much to protect the volunteer from lawsuits, it is not a guarantee that lawsuits will not take place against you or the volunteer. As with any law, it can be challenged. This is why it is best to sit down with a lawyer and an insurance agent and go over all of the contingencies. What you do not want to do is just avoid the whole issue by not developing a robust volunteer program. Doing so means you are abandoning a great resource that can be a great help and support to you and your staff in providing excellent, person-centered care. And looking at the incident rates for volunteers involved in lawsuits, one finds they are few and far between. They are certainly far, far less than the current number of lawsuits against professional staff. Again, (I apologize for sounding like a broken record), with professional volunteer leadership, vetting, and training "super" volunteers, will add a great deal in your favor of risk management. You are eliminating those persons, up front, who may not have the desire or capacity to meet your "super" expectations. At the same time your cautious and comprehensive approach will result in a volunteer force that has the desire and capacity to meet your "super" expectations. Sustainability is directly connected to this discussion on liability.

"Volunteer programs are not sustainable, and volunteers are not reliable."

The second excuse I hear when I talk about expanding the role of volunteers goes something like this: "Volunteer programs are not sustainable because volunteers are just not reliable." In instances where the volunteer program only receives a perfunctory nod, that may be true. But under what circumstances were the volunteers recruited? What were the expectations of the potential volunteer? Who was the person that was recruiting them? Were they a full-time professional volunteer manager or someone from your staff who wears many hats? What screening process took place? What training did the potential volunteer receive? And finally, what on-going training and professional oversight, if any, was provided?

As I have mentioned previously, hiring a professional volunteer coordinator is essential for increasing the likelihood that the volunteer program will be successful, effective, and most importantly, sustainable. When you look at examples of great programs as we will do in Chapter Seven, the first item to note is that these programs have several things in common. First, the person directing the program has received formal education in the management of volunteer programs and volunteers. Successful programs do not just happen by luck. The administrator views the director of volunteers as a critical manager in the operation of the nursing home. That director works in tandem with the care staff managers to ensure the bio-pyscho-social needs of the residents are fully met. Successful programs are well thought out and well executed.

There are likely several tracks for engaging volunteers. The most informal track is "walk-in" volunteers. They saw something on social media, or they heard or saw something in the newspaper, or they saw an ad on television or some other form of media, and decided, pretty much on a whim, to show up at your nursing home "to do something." Most likely, they will return for some time, but when the emotional response subsides, they go off to pursue another opportunity "to do something else." This is not a bad thing; that walk-in volunteers may discover a true passion for working with older adults and return in the future with a deeper level of commitment.

Volunteering awoke my passion for older adults, drawing me into this world. I went to the nursing home to perform music for the people, and I never looked back. So, walk-ins are great, but they are not your bread and butter, they are not your "super" volunteer, at least not yet.

The next level of volunteers are those volunteers that come for special occasions, i.e., birthdays, anniversaries, sing-a-longs, worship services or game playing activities. They may come once a month or during the holidays. Of course, December is a notorious time for being the month when "everyone" decides to come and sing Christmas carols. It's all good, but these are not your "super" volunteers.

I have to pause here for just a minute to share a funny story with you. It happened in the days just before Christmas. I arrived at a nursing home to play Christmas carols, only to discover that I was one of many entertainers that had come that day. They came to play and sing Christmas carols, one after another, all day long. I'm sure the entertainers, as well as myself, had pure motives. We wanted the people to experience the joy of the season. When it was my turn to play, I entered the room packed with residents, family, children, and staff, but as I entered the room, and within ear-shot and unbeknownst to her, I heard an older woman say, "If I hear Joy to the World one more time today, I'll scream." I thought to myself, "Ok, I'll skip that one." The point is, anytime someone is coming in to provide group activities is a good thing, but they may come only periodically, or even only once, never to be seen again. These are not your "super" volunteers either.

And then you have volunteers that possibly serve on your board of directors, auxiliaries, and volunteers that help you raise funds for the nursing home. These volunteers may or may not have ongoing contact with your residents, but they are essential to the success of your operations. If they have taken on the responsibility for guiding the activities of the nursing home, they are great volunteers, but the "super" volunteer is a different breed. Recruiting for and screening for the "super" volunteer is where you find a person who understands that consistency and commitment are paramount to you, your staff, and most importantly to the people for whom you care.

Volunteers at this "super" level are highly committed individuals who are passionate about serving older adults. They are self-starters who are successful in whatever career path they've chosen. They are "other-person" focused, which goes to person-centered care. These "super" volunteers are able and willing to learn new skills. They thrive under good leadership, and most important, they are looking for meaningful ways to give back to the communities in which they live. If your program is not well organized, is poorly planned, and is not under the oversight of a "great" director of volunteers, these "super volunteers" will move on until they find the opportunity in which they can express their desires and talents, with appreciation in return. These people are reliable; in fact, your staff will be amazed at just how committed they are to the staff and to the people for whom you care. I have been asked many times by nursing home administrators and staff, "Where do you find these people?" The answer is simple. You design your program to attract "these" people, as I discuss in detail in Chapter Eight. In short, you start by developing a screening and vetting process that filters for persons who have those attributes I've mentioned, i.e., highly committed, passionate, desirous and intellectually capable of learning new skills, "others" oriented, and they are looking for a well-structured program in which they can become a member.

In some of the examples I highlight later in the book, you will find that these "super" volunteers go on to assume even greater responsibility for various aspects of the volunteer program. During one of my initial conversations with Syrelle Bernstein (personal interview, May 15, 2016), the director of volunteers, (now retired) at Baycrest Health Sciences in Toronto, I asked her questions about the Baycrest volunteer program. During our conversation, she relayed to me that even at that moment while we were talking on the telephone, she had trained volunteers conducting volunteer interviews and screening for new volunteer candidates.

In taking a more in-depth look into the Baycrest volunteer program, you will discover that volunteers are operating at all the levels I mentioned above, plus other areas such as program development and research. So, with all that said, not only is the Baycrest volunteer program sustainable, the volunteers reliable, but the Baycrest volunteers are also bringing innovative programming and research to the table. Once more, this and other examples clearly demonstrate that with serious investment and proper resourcing, volunteer programs in nursing homes are sustainable and the volunteers are reliable. Moreover, they are innovative.

"Volunteers will replace paid employees."

When nursing home staff see that the volunteer program is being ramped up to become a credible entity within the nursing home, they may begin to worry, and rightly so, that they are being replaced with "free labor." Your professional care staff needs to be included in the planning and execution of the volunteer program so that you have their buy-in from the beginning of the process. To begin, they need to understand what the role of the "super" volunteer will be, what the expectations of these volunteers will be, what the boundaries will be for the "super" volunteers, and how the screening and training processes will take place. If the nursing home staff is included in the process right from the beginning, then there will be less pushback from the staff in the days ahead. However, in talking with administrators that have instituted robust volunteer programs, I learned administrators can anticipate some staff attrition. The administrators I have interviewed have all said the effort was worth the pain. As a result of holding firmly to the principles of the "super" volunteer force, they have created a tremendous, integrated workforce, made up of both paid and unpaid people. The volunteers are intrinsic to the day-to-day life of the nursing home. The staff and volunteers work, not as two separate groups, but as a single and integrated team delivering care.

When labor unions are involved, there have to be clear expectations set as to what the volunteers will and will not do; this applies to the paid employees as well. Employers cannot coerce employees to "volunteer" their skills and time. If an employee wants to volunteer time to the nursing home, it should be in an area outside of their regular day-to-day work, and it should be made abundantly clear to everyone involved that the goal is not to replace paid staff with unpaid staff.

The "super" volunteer has not been and will not be trained to provide medical cares or provide personal tasks such as toileting and bathing, which are just two activities of daily living. In the future, this may change if the staffing shortage continues to worsen. "Super" volunteers may have to be trained to provide some of these cares, as there will not be enough professional staff on hand. But for now, the goal is to create a cadre of volunteers that have been trained to provide one-on-one relationships with the residents to address feelings of loneliness, to gain insight into each person's desires, and to learn what matters most to the older adults with whom they are spending time. Those insights provided by the volunteer can go a long way to informing care plans to include interventions that may reduce or even eliminate negative behaviors, thereby reducing staff workload.

Without question, volunteers can be trained to work alongside staff to provide support with the intent of lifting some of the workload. When a nurse highly skilled in technical care is dressing someone, is that a good use of already scarce resources (Litwak, 1985)? I think not. Can a volunteer be trained to help people rise in the morning, dress, and groom for the day? I think so. I know so. Can volunteers be trained to assist with feeding? Yes, the Silver Spoons volunteers trained to provide feeding assistance in the United States (Musson, Frye & Nash, 1997) demonstrate that this is more than possible. In fact, the program has enjoyed great success and has transformed mealtime from a "hurry up and let's get them fed," to a leisurely social event in which the resident and the volunteer enjoy each other's company (Harvey, Coulter, Zublena, & Woodard, 2013). John, a Silver Spoon volunteer, takes great satisfaction and pride in knowing that the time he spends helping a nursing home resident eat results in that resident eating most of their meal at each sitting, rather than just sitting and staring at their food.

On the other hand, employees should not be required to "volunteer" some of their time. Over the years, I have had nurses come to me desiring to volunteer at a nursing home, but not where they are employed. The nurses I've spoken with expressed to me that they entered the nursing profession because they wanted to help people. Instead, because of onerous federal and state regulations, they spend a majority of their time behind a desk charting resident activity and completing mountains of paperwork. I caution them to keep in mind that when they go to the nursing home to volunteer, they are not a nurse, they are volunteers. In the same vein, if a nurse wants to volunteer at the nursing facility where she works, she may neither engage in, nor be compelled by her employer to participate in, cares that mirror part of her usual, day-to-day, paid nursing duties.

Years ago, I heard a guest speaker say, "Remember to keep the main thing, the main thing." I think those words apply here. I hope what everyone desires, hopes for, works towards, is that the people living in our nursing homes are getting high-quality care and experiencing a rich quality of life that is positive and fulfilling. Therefore, in those talks with labor union leaders, with staff and management, let's keep the main thing, the main thing.

Finally, staff needs reassurance that this new level of volunteer effort is not an attempt to replace them with unpaid staff. Instead, the staff should be trained to understand the intent of creating this cadre of "super" volunteers. From there, the paid staff can develop a list of tasks where volunteers could assist the staff. Is it helping make beds, helping with dressing and grooming, feeding assistance, and so on? Then let the staff train the volunteer in how to complete those tasks. The nurses can train the volunteers how to dress and groom people. The dietitians and the speech pathologists can train volunteers to provide meal assistance and so on. This way, the staff knows what the volunteer has been trained to do, that the volunteer has been properly trained, and the staff can assist in monitoring the volunteer performing those tasks. For example, in one nursing home, where volunteers are assisting with feeding, the dietitian and speech pathologist trained the volunteers to correctly position the resident, adjust the rate of feeding, the amount of food offered with each bite, and to look for signs of discomfort. It works very well. Once the staff realizes how valuable these "super" volunteers are, they become an indispensable part of the care team. One staff member said, "We could not do what we are doing without them [the volunteers]."

"Policy prohibits volunteers from making valuable contributions to the residents or staff."

This is another myth. In most cases, policy such as the Omnibus Budget Reconciliation Act of 1987 (OBRA '87) does not prohibit volunteers from providing meaningful support for staff. What the regulations do say is that volunteers cannot provide support of activities of daily living (ADLs). Only certified nursing assistants (CNAs) and nurses can provide this assistance (Moss & Remsburg, 2005). ADLs include: 1) feeding, 2) dressing, 3) grooming, 4) bathing, 5) toileting, and 6) transferring, i.e., being about to move from the bed to the wheelchair and vice versa. In light of the staffing shortages, it's time to re-think the potential of well-trained volunteers.

What is needed is a serious review of this list of activities to permit well-screened and trained volunteers to dress someone properly, to groom someone, and as we've already seen, provide feeding assistance. Much of these limitations of what a volunteer can and cannot do are based upon the professional care provider's definition of what is and isn't "medical" care. Re-evaluating what can only be done by a medical professional and what can be done by a "super" volunteer can result in a significant improvement in the use of the professional's time (Moss & Remsburg, 2005). The goal is to open the doors to a resource that can more than adequately address not only the emotional and social needs of the people living in nursing homes, but also some of their physical needs as well.

"Volunteer programs are expensive and, in the end, produce very little output."

I'm sure you know the saying, "You get what you pay for." Additionally, you may be familiar with President Theodore Roosevelt's observation, upon his return to the United States from his attempted negotiations with Columbia, "'I was forced to conclude that to endeavor to negotiate with Columbia was about like trying to nail currant jelly to the wall. You can't do it. It isn't the fault of the nail; it's the fault of the jelly'" (Richardson, 1921, p. 34).

Similarly, I will conclude that measuring the return on your investment in a volunteer program is complicated; it not only includes the tangibles, like fewer falls or reducing the use of psychotropic medications, but it also includes intangibles, like improved quality of life and enhanced community image. To paraphrase Roosevelt, "It's not the fault of the survey instrument, it's the fault of the construct." The measuring of happiness, life-satisfaction, quality of life and yes, even quality of care, results in values that can be challenged. However, there is hope. The research focused on measuring the return on the investment indicates that volunteer programs do indeed produce a hefty return on investment. Femida Handy, Ph.D., Professor, University of Pennsylvania, and Director of the School of Social Policy and Practice, has written extensively on this topic, studying the challenge of measuring volunteer benefits versus program costs and the value of volunteers to an institution, (Handy & Mook, 2011; Handy & Srinivasan, 2004).

In her 2004 study, Handy, evaluating thirty-one hospitals in the Toronto area, found, on average, the return on investment (ROI) value of the volunteer was $6.84 for every dollar that the hospital had spent on the volunteer program. This was a 684% ROI. Each of the hospitals had hired a professional director of volunteers to manage the program, and each hospital had at least 100 volunteers, ranging all the way to 3,240 volunteers, with an average of 700 volunteers in each hospital. The average size of hospitals in the sample was 468 beds.

The people managing the volunteer programs were professionals; they had formal training in volunteer programming and volunteer management (which is key to program success). In addition to surveying the management teams of the hospitals, the researchers interviewed the volunteers and the staff. This data provided a rich pool of information that would go on to inform this study. The majority of the volunteers were female, with half of them retired and half having completed post-secondary education, which I also have found to be a typical demographic.

Volunteers in the hospitals were used to supplement staff by providing some relief through giving non-medical care, while adding a "human and personal" touch. Volunteers provided one-on-one companionship, assisted with group activities, escorted or helped patients get from one place to another, shopped for needed items, provided support to families, and assisted with the behind the scenes tasks such as clerical and other administrative tasks (Handy & Srinivasan, 2004).

During researcher interviews with the hospital managers, the theme, "improving and maintaining community relations," emerged repeatedly. Community relations was of great value to managers who recognized that volunteers were not only successful in recruiting new volunteers and even attracting new paid staff, but the volunteers also were successful in encouraging community donations to the hospital. Volunteers raised the profile of the hospital in the community's eyes. How valuable is your nursing home profile to the community? Sadly, due to the media's propensity to headline tragic and dramatic news, the common perception of the nursing home is that terrible place where people get hurt and a place that should be avoided at all costs. However, well trained "super" volunteers become ambassadors to your community, carrying a different message, a message that says there is another side to the nursing home story. The "super" volunteer is in an excellent position to impact the resident's sense of dignity and self-worth, while improving the quality of life through nurturing personal relationships with the residents. In this process, the volunteers become intimately familiar with your residents' stories and histories, as well as witnessing first-hand the tremendous effort your staff is making to ensure your residents are getting good care. From there they go into the community with better news. So how do we go about measuring the value of the volunteer program's ROI?

Measuring the ROI of your volunteer program begins with calculating the value of the services your volunteers are providing. Every year, the Independent Sector[2], an organization whose members represent foundations, volunteer organizations, and even companies giving programs, estimates the value of the volunteer hour (based on the average wages of all non-farm workers' payroll and add 12 percent to account for benefits). At the time of this writing, the value of the volunteer hour is estimated to be $24.14. As an example, if you were to have 100 volunteers working in your nursing home for about two hours per week or 104 hours per year (a very conservative estimate), then the volunteers would have provided 10,400 hours of service. Multiplying 10,400 by $24.14 equals $251,056 in the value of donated volunteer hours. However, volunteers in many cases are

---

[2] https://www.independentsector.org/resource/the-value-of-volunteer-time/

giving far more than just their time. Their donation may include the costs of childcare while volunteering, transportation costs traveling to and from your facility. Their contribution even includes the value of their leisure time given up for volunteering time. Handy and Mook (2011) report that the volunteers they studied reported about $317 in annual expenses, but when "opportunity costs" were added (i.e., lost wages of about 340 hours), the average number of hours volunteers gave, multiplied by $14, (an average wage per hour), the total amount realized for each volunteer was more like $4,763! This amount goes into the calculation of the value of the volunteer program as well. So, in the end, if we have 100 volunteers donating some $4,763 annually, plus the value of their time while at your nursing home, the collective value of those 100 volunteers is $727,356!

If volunteer program costs average $80,000 per year, and I'm including the wages of the director of volunteers, benefits and operating costs, then the ratio between cost per dollar versus volunteer value per hour would be roughly $1: $9. For every dollar you spend on the volunteer program, the volunteers are producing $9 in donated services, a 900% return on your investment. If you were to have 700 volunteers as in the Handy (2011) study referred to above, that would be volunteers giving two hours per week for one year, then the value of their services would be $1,757,392 or a ratio then roughly 1:22 or a 2,200% return on your investment! Of course, if you have 700 volunteers, you will likely have an assistant to the director of volunteers as well which would raise the cost to about $120,000 per year, in which case the ratio would be 1:14.6. But my point is made.

The ratio of cost to value is known as the VIVA ratio. Katherine Gaskin (2011) of the Institute of Volunteering Research (IVR) has developed a tool helpful in determining the "VIVA" ratio. You can find a link to this tool in the reference section of this book. But this is not the end of the calculating.

Now that we have the tangible values calculated, what of calculating the value of all those difficult-to-measure intangibles, I mentioned above. What is the value of your nursing home's image in the community? What is the value of residents feeling better about themselves, about quality of life? What is the value of residents not hitting the call lights so often or creating circumstances that pull staff away from their work? And then what about those quality measures that determine your star rating? How much is your star rating impacting your budget? What about the impact your volunteers are having on your staff's sense of job satisfaction or staff retention rates? You must consider all of these factors as they affect the ROI of your volunteer program as well. It's not an easy task but making an effort to arrive at these values will, I am confident, clearly show that the investment in a robust volunteer program produces a significant return on investment.

In their 2011 study, Handy and Mook took on the task of quantifying the intangible benefits of volunteer programs. First, they state that organizations, to have an effective and "optimal" volunteer program, need to treat the volunteer program as they would any other potential resource by calculating the cost-benefit of the program. However, they point out that organizations fail to do this, seeing the volunteer program as an optional add-on that does not require this sort of scrutiny. Understanding the value of these intangibles from both the organization's and the volunteers' perspective improves the sustainability of the program (Handy & Mook, 2011).

One tactic for measuring the intangibles is to use surrogate constructs or proxy variables that reflect the value of an intangible. The proxy variables act as mirrors, in that we can't measure the intangible directly, but we can measure its impact on a variety of items such as incident rates for falls, urinary tract infections, use of psychotropic drugs, and staff retention rates and job satisfaction scores, volunteer feedback and so on. As an example, how would we go about measuring the quality of life of a resident? Just asking someone to rate their quality of life by picking a value from 1 to 10, on a scale where 1 is "very poor" and 10 is "very good" would not really indicate whether the person understood the term "quality of life." If they are giving what they think is the response being sought after by the interviewer; and third, even when the resident responds to the question with the best of intentions, how do we know what an "8" really represents? Furthermore, between residents, what does an "8" mean? One person's "8" may be "10" for another person. So, we are in a quandary of sorts. However, we could ask them questions about their day-to-day experience in the nursing home and from their responses ascertain if they have a positive quality of life. We could ask questions about their activities of daily living (ADL): are they eating? do they enjoy their meals? are they participating in the activities they like? and do they feel as if someone cares about them? We could go a step further and ask the staff questions similar to the questions we asked the resident. Is Mrs. Smith eating her meals? Does she complain about the food? Is she engaging in activities that she enjoys? Does she ever express her feelings about the care she is receiving? And so, the aggregation of these responses paints a picture of the resident experience, i.e., quality of life. However, how does that translate into dollars and cents?

If people are not happy, how does that impact the budget? If people are not eating, or the incident rate for out-of-character responses, urinary tract infections, use of psychotropic drugs, and/or pressure sores are on the increase, what is the impact to the budget?

For each of the intangibles, resident satisfaction, community involvement, quality of life, we need to find indicators, i.e., proxy variables that will allow us to approximate quantifiable monetary values to estimate the value of the volunteer program. Anecdotally, I think we know that social contact has a positive impact on the nursing home resident but what is the value of that impact? It takes some work to identify those indicators but, in the end, we arrive at a more accurate picture of the cost-benefit of the volunteer program. So, in the end, we can determine the value of "hard" tangibles and approximate the value of the "soft" intangibles using proxy variables or indicators to give us a more accurate picture of the volunteer program ROI. There are other methods and tools for determining the value of the volunteer program.

Goulbourne and Embuldeniya (2002) present eight tools for estimating the value of the volunteer program. Each of the eight tools reports either the value of the volunteer hour and volunteer activity. They compare the volunteer value to the value of a paid employee using relative wages for a particular task and include the paid volunteer's benefits as well. A volunteer hour may be assigned a value of $11 per hour based on the work they are performing, and then a percentage of that $11, 15 percent, for example, is added to the $11 to account for the equivalency of benefits if the volunteer were a paid employee. They also present reporting ratio such as the Community Investment Ratio which compares the nursing home investment into the volunteer program with the investment volunteers have made into the program. Also, they provide formulas for calculating how many full-time employees it would take to replace the number of volunteer hours donated.

To once again make my intentions clear, my purpose is not to promote the idea of replacing paid professional staff with volunteers but to strongly encourage you, the manager of a long-term care community, to take your volunteer program seriously and invest in it to provide additional support for your professional staff. These tools are available online and I would encourage directors of volunteers to make use of them in reporting the value of your volunteer program.

To conclude this chapter, let me encourage you to seek professional help in developing a robust volunteer program. With the staffing shortage as it is, with little or no sign of change, as well as the attack on Medicare and Medicaid funding and funding for the Older American's Act, which provides many vital services for older adults, we need to "involve" the community at large. If we do not, how can we hope to provide good care?

There is beauty in the simplicity of a positive response: there are people in our communities who, if they knew the challenges that you are facing as an administrator, director of nursing, social worker, activities director, and direct care workers, would step in to provide meaningful help. But and this is a big point, you cannot do it halfway. Seek out someone who has the training and experience of managing volunteers and then resource them. I am sure that whatever dollars you spend on the front-end of this effort will come back to you ten-fold. I realize that budgets are tight, but things are not going to get better. Engaging the community is not a silver bullet, but it will undoubtedly go a long way in relieving some of the pressures you face.

Putting your "super" volunteer program together requires careful planning, and addressing each of the challenges presented here. Involve your staff right from the beginning in the development process. Allow your team to help shape a program that has everyone's buy-in, while recognizing that you may experience some attrition. Hire a "great" director of volunteers then launch the program. Following these steps will lead to what Jill's staff concluded after 18 months into the program, "We couldn't do what we are doing without our volunteers."

CHAPTER SIX

It Can Be Done. Really, It Can Be Done!

———

"Believe it can be done. When you believe something can be done, really believe, your mind will find the ways to do it. Believing a solution paves the way to solution."

— DAVID J. SCHWARTZ

(author, *The Magic of Thinking Big*)

I ESPECIALLY LOOKED FORWARD to writing this chapter. It was exciting for me to search out and discover (while writing the previous five chapters) long-term care providers in various parts of the globe that share a similar vision for using volunteers in expanded roles.

These providers have created what I consider to be exemplary programs which other providers can research and emulate. One of the common factors among them is their leadership's authentic zeal for providing not just for the physical needs of their residents, but also for supporting their emotional and social needs. In talking with them, it also became clear to me that they understood that the business of caring for older adults is two-thirds relationship building and one-third medical treatment.

I hope that as I introduce you to these programs and the people who created and manage them, you will be inspired and encouraged to pursue building a "super" volunteer program made up of "super" volunteers who will be a work-ready resource for you.

The four programs that I present here were (at the time of this writing) in various stages of development, with Roskilde Nursing Home in Kristiansund, Norway the newest program of the four, and Baycrest being, in my estimation, the most advanced. Arcare of Australia is doing some remarkable things with their residents, thanks to Daniella Greenwood, Strategy and Innovation Manager. Daniella also provides us with great insight into what person-centered care really means. Jill Woodward, CEO of the Elizabeth-Knox Nursing Home in Auckland, New Zealand drives home the fact that a well-trained director of volunteers plays an indispensable role in creating a significant and sustainable volunteer program. The Knox Nursing Home has 192 beds supported by professional care staff and 700 to 800 volunteers! Before I introduce you to Jill, I would like to start with the Roskilde Nursing Home in Kristiansund, Norway, where we will learn what led to the development of their program, how their volunteer program was conceived, and finally, how they implemented the volunteer program.

Roskilde Nursing Home, Kristiansund kommune, Norway

To start on this exploration and discovery of exemplary volunteer programs in nursing homes, I created several social media accounts. I found Twitter to be most useful, as well as Hootsuite, (social media management software). Both apps allowed me to track multiple keywords, create lists and ultimately to meet people who shared a similar vision for expanding the role of volunteers in nursing homes. Also, I created the blog VolunCheerLeader.com with the help of my good friends, MJ & Caroline McBride of Rebel Interactive. I took time every day, (and I still do) to search keywords such as "nursing home volunteers" "volunteers" "nursing homes" and any other relevant terms that came to my mind. It paid off; in the first few weeks, a link to an article came to me through Twitter. The article was a case study by Service Design Network entitled "Volunteer Service for Nursing Home Residents Reimagines Social Care System."[3] The article explained how Emilie Strommen Olsen, senior program designer for DesignIt and retained by Roskilde Nursing Home had developed a volunteer program for the nursing home. The Norwegian government designated development centers in each of its counties. Roskilde was one of the designated centers. Their purpose was to explore better ways to care for older adults. I emailed Emilie immediately and arranged a Skype interview with her and Stephanie Helland, the unit manager of the Roskilde Nursing Home.

Recall that Dr. Bill Thomas (1996) talked about the "three plagues of the nursing home, boredom, uselessness, and loneliness." These were the same plagues the residents at Roskilde Nursing Home were facing. The residents were not engaged. They sat, day in and day out, with little activity or stimulation. The residents' inactivity was the result of Roskilde's facing serious workforce challenges, like every other long-term care provider in the world.

Consequently, the care staff of Roskilde was working very hard just to meet the basic needs of the residents. They did not have time for much more. The staff recognized, however, that the residents needed more than just medical care and staff members were feeling frustrated and saddened that they were not able to offer that level of personal care. Emilie's interviews with staff revealed their remorse and their feelings of guilt because they felt they were not

---

[3] A link to the article was posted on Twitter. The article dated June 19, 2018 can be found at https://www.service-design-network. org/case-studies/volunteer-service-for-nursing-home-residents# however, access is restricted to members of the Service Design Network (SDN).

doing enough. The staff felt that they could not give the people what they most needed—their time and friendship. The families of the residents expressed the same sense of helplessness and frustration asking as one of the family members asked: "Can't someone do something about this?"

Because Roskilde was a development center, Stephanie, the administrator, had the resources to do something about this and she did. She contacted DesignIt, a global design firm with offices around the world, including Oslo, Norway. It was then that Emilie took on the challenge of designing a volunteer program for Roskilde. She began by asking the staff, the residents, and their families: "What kind of volunteer services do you want?" Through focus groups and in-depth interviews, the answer was crystal clear: "We want just one person to talk to and do "normal" stuff, not big activities where everyone participates at once." (By the way, the resident's desire for "just one person to talk to," is a recurring theme I heard as I interviewed volunteer coordinators in other care homes).

With this input, Emilie's team went to work, using the information she received from the three stakeholders: the resident, the staff, and families. It was critical that the staff be involved in this process early on, to garner their support for this effort. Reflecting on the process, Emilie stated, "It was really one of the success factors, that at the start, the staff was involved all the time during the process…so that they felt that they owned it." (Olsen, personal interview, February 23, 2016). They launched the pilot program in the fall of 2014, and after evaluations and with "brilliant" feedback from the participants, according to Stephanie, the *Trivselvenn i sykehjem*, (translated: Buddy Service in nursing homes) service was launched in January 2015.

Emilie developed a matrix with staff member positions in rows and responsibilities in the columns. Everyone had a role to play in the process, from interviewing the volunteer candidates to orienting them to the nursing home environment, to assigning them to an area of the nursing home, and finally, to the staff and volunteers meeting periodically for follow-up. Stephanie said that the implementation was very smooth. She laughed and said, *"It was almost done without anyone noticing!"* A large chart was posted for all to see informing both the staff and volunteers of their responsibilities, who would be volunteering that week, and who they would be visiting.

During the test period, Stephanie did hear concerns from the staff that the volunteers might be taking over their tasks and thus eliminating the need for paid staff. She assured them that this was not the case. The volunteers were there to give emotional support and engage the residents in meaningful activities that would promote their sense of well-being and quality of life. Once the staff understood what was happening, they began to realize that the volunteer was indeed providing welcomed relief.

Emilie and Stephanie highlighted some critical lessons learned during this process:

1. Volunteers want to feel welcomed and appreciated.

2. Volunteers want to be guided by the staff.

As a result, one of the volunteer positions is the "volunteer greeter." As volunteers arrive for their visit, a veteran volunteer greets them! Each volunteer wears a button that has a red heart on it, symbolizing this is a volunteer. The professional staff wear buttons with a blue heart. I asked Stephanie to describe the typical volunteer. She explained that they are getting people of all ages, from 16 years of age and up, including mothers on maternity leave who wanted to feel still like they could make a difference, and retirees who brought their skills and expertise to their volunteer experience. Volunteers bringing their skills and expertise is a recurring theme throughout my interviews with nursing home staff.

One volunteer explained that he was in the process of looking for a new job, one that would not interfere with his nursing home visits. *"Volunteering is an emerging concept in Norway,"* said Emilie. "Places like Britain have a long, rich history of volunteerism, but for us, it is a new trend. People are asking: 'How can I be a resource?' 'How can I give to my society?'"

Finally, I asked Stephanie if the volunteer program had made a real impact. "Definitely! We've seen changes in our residents. One of our patients with dementia will talk even hours later about the visit she had with her 'buddy.' Other patients will say 'Today my buddy is coming to visit me, only me, just to me...'" Hearing this statement reminded me of an older woman who observed during one of my visits with her, "I have a lot of people around me, nurses, aides, but there is no one here just for me." I believe we have all experienced that feeling one time or another.

For the staff, Stephanie said there had been a definite change in the way they think about volunteers. "They told me, 'If we are going to prioritize some positions, we have to prioritize a volunteer coordinator because that is such important work. We'd rather you prioritize the volunteer coordinator than a nurse.'" Now, that reflects a significant paradigm shift!

For me, it was a great thrill to see this group discover the positive impact volunteers can have on the staff, on the people for whom they care, and on their families and loved ones. It is important to note that the success of this program was due to querying the stakeholders, collecting their ideas, careful program development to address the expressed needs of the stakeholders, and then gaining the confidence of the staff through their involvement in program development from the very beginning. Finally, hiring a trained volunteer manager was critical.

Arcare—Australia

It all started when someone tweeted the link to a video entitled, "It Takes a Community."[4] Curious, I clicked on the link to watch it. The video started like many promotional videos, but about 30 seconds into this video, I realized there was something extraordinary happening at Arcare. The interviews reflected a sincerity and authenticity that were unmistakable. I was riveted by the participants' passion and love for the people they were serving. Over and over, each person in the video repeated how important relationship was to providing quality care. As the video ended, an older woman, an Arcare resident, stated, "Laughter is great therapy." By the end of the video, I was moved to tears.

Immediately, I went to the Arcare website and contacted Daniella Greenwood, Strategy and Innovation manager for Arcare Aged Care. Daniella had appeared in the video. We connected and what I thought would be about a 45-minute interview turned into a 90-minute exchange of experiences, laughter, a few tears and learning about Arcare's philosophy of care.

To begin, throughout the video, Daniella Greenwood repeatedly reiterated that "...nurturing relationships between staff, families, and residents, is the most important thing we do." Coincidently, I was then researching and writing a workshop on the topic of person-centered care, (see Chapter Four). Listening to Daniella, it became clear to me that person-centered care was not just about discovering when someone wanted to rise or what they would like to eat for breakfast, or in which activities they would like to participate. Rather, as Tom Kitwood's (1997) original intent made clear, person-centered care required not only knowing a person's prefer-

---

4 "It Takes a Community" retrieved from https://www.youtube.com/watch?v=IUJWFWXz-wY

ences but it also meant nurturing a culture of relationships between all of the stakeholders, i.e., staff to resident, staff to volunteer, staff to families, staff to staff, volunteer to volunteer, resident to resident, and every other combination. Person-centered care includes nurturing a culture in which staff can move beyond their traditional training of keeping a professional distance, to permitting them to bring their "humanness" to work with them, (Greenwood, personal interview, November 6, 2016).

Let me illustrate this concept further. Having received training in giving person-centered care, a nurse aide has waited until the resident has finished their afternoon nap to give the resident their medications. As the nurse aide enters the room, pleasant conversation is exchanged. The nurse aide may ask if the resident enjoyed their nap while the nurse aide is careful to address the resident as they wish. They may even exchange more light conversation, but then the nurse aide's agenda emerges, "I, (the nurse aide), am here primarily not to visit with you or attend to your emotional or social needs, but rather I am here because I need you to do something for me." The resident senses that the nurse did not initiate the meeting out of a personal concern for "me," but rather the need to complete a task. Granted, it is terrific that the nurse aide is following what she has been taught, but it is not the end of the story, as Daniella points out in the video: "…old people are vulnerable, and they need critical support and assistance but that's one small part of what they need, the rest of it's called life."[5]

Life, what is that? What is life for *the person living in a nursing home?* As the resident said to me, "I have a lot of people around me, but there is no one here just for me." "…just for me…" What

---

[5] "It Takes a Community" retrieved from https://www.youtube.com/watch?v=IUJWFWXz-wY

does this mean? What is the need this person is expressing? Daniella explained it this way "…it's about context, real people in real relationships in a social world, hanging out together. Life is what happens during the care, the task, whatever is going on, everything can become a moment of connection. This [moment of connection] leads to the natural creation of genuine friendship." (personal interview, November 7, 2016).

The result for Daniella was that they have moved beyond "person-centered" language to a culture where staff, volunteers, families, and residents become best friends, hanging out together, doing things together off the clock, even taking trips to the beach, or the resident going home with a staff member for a home-cooked meal. They called it the "Buddy" program, an idea conceived by Karen Watt, manager of Helensvale, one of several Arcare communities. It was no longer about "us" and "them" it's just about "us."

Surprised by the many positive comments she was getting about her house cleaner, Daniella asked, "I kept hearing about these fantastic relationships that the residents had with the cleaning staff. What is it about these relationships?' The resident said to me 'It's just a normal relationship.' I said, 'Guess what?' the house cleaner is probably one of the few people who is not trying to take her [the resident's] clothes off or have seen her in her most private moments. It's just a normal relationship. They are friends." (Greenwood, personal interview, November 6, 2016).

Daniella, realizing that cultivating an environment where relationships would be key, knew that nurses coming from acute settings such as hospitals, where patients may only be with the nurse for a few days, were likely encouraged to keep a "professional" distance from the patient. When the nurse arrived at the nursing home to work, she may bring that same mentality with her and pass that on to the personal care workers. However, in the nursing home setting, keeping a distance does not make sense as the residents may be with the staff for years. With that, Daniella was set to provide training for the nursing staff. She met a great deal of resistance until she had an epiphany moment.

One afternoon, Daniella happened to overhear a conversation just around the corner from where she stood; she could not see the people talking. What she was hearing was a mother praising and encouraging her children. The two children had come to the nursing home to see their mother after school. Daniella stated, "It wasn't earth-shattering, but it was this gorgeous conversation. She was really boosting their self-esteem. One of them had had a bad day at school. I poked my head around the corner and looked. And there was one of those care staff members who I thought was a monster with all of these skills that I was just about to train: empathy, noticing, presence. She had it! Then I felt a combination of shame and epiphany. And I thought, 'Wait a minute. She doesn't need to be trained to bring this to work with her. She just needs permission.'"

From that point forward, the culture at Arcare evolved from person-centered care to relationship-centered care based on the Senses Framework (Mike Nolan, 2006). (See Chapter Four for a discussion of the Senses Framework).

If, at this point, you are wondering what this all has to do with creating "super" volunteers, the answer is simply, "Everything." All the topics I have been promoting concerning "super" volunteers revolve around nurturing relationships. Daniella confirmed for me that there is something well beyond just knowing a person's preferences. What we need to know is what the older adult cares about, what matters to them. Do they feel secure? Do they feel connected? Do they have a sense of purpose? Are they given opportunities to grow? And finally, are they experiencing joy, not occasionally, but on a continuing basis? This is the beginning of relationship-centered living. "Super" volunteers are in a great position to be trained to offer that level of care.

Elizabeth-Knox Nursing Home—Auckland, New Zealand

Dr. Allen Power came to Omaha to speak about the use of antipsychotics and dementia. He had recently released his second book, *Dementia Beyond Disease* (2017a). After his presentation, I introduced myself and explained as briefly as I could, (and for me that is a challenge), my goal to promote expanding the role of the volunteer in nursing homes. He was very gracious and invited me to contact him so that he could introduce me to people he believed would be sympathetic to this cause. Dr. Power introduced me to Jill Woodward, CEO of Elizabeth-Knox Nursing Home. To my amazement, he announced, "She has a 140-bed nursing home and 800 volunteers!" I knew, at that moment, I had to contact Jill and find out more about her volunteer program. It took a few weeks of emailing and figuring out the best time to connect, as Auckland was 17 hours ahead of me in Nebraska. When we did finally connect, as you might expect, it was a great conversation. Her energy, zeal, and passion for providing quality care came through loud and clear over the thousands of miles of communication electronics. Here is a portion of our conversation, along with comments emailed to me by Kristen O'Reilly, hired by Jill as the first Volunteer Coordinator for the Knox home. Kristen is now the Community Partnerships Manager for Knox and is mentoring two volunteer coordinators.

Excerpts from my conversation with Jill on August 30, 2016

> **Paul:** I was talking with Dr. Allen Power, and he told me that you have a great volunteer program. I'm writing a book that advocates for expanding the role of volunteers in nursing homes. And so, I'd like to talk with you about your volunteer program.

Jill: Volunteers play a really big part of what we do here. We've had our program up and running for about three years now. The first thing we did was recruit a really great volunteer coordinator! One of the things we did was to create a volunteer program that focuses on the critical need for resident companionship. We have 700 to 800 volunteers. We've never had an expectation that volunteers would do what staff members are doing. But we do have volunteers that work alongside team leaders when they first come to work at Knox, so they have a sense of confidence about what they are doing.

Paul: Do you have a formal training program for them?

Jill: We do indeed. We have a volunteer coordinator [Kristen O'Reilly] that we first engaged whose role has now changed to "Community Partnership Manager." We hired two new volunteer coordinators, Monica, and Margaret, who work all seven days because we cover the weekend, as well to support our volunteers. We have a really extensive training program available for Knox volunteers. The process of recruitment involves a one-on-one interview with one of our two fabulous coordinators Monica or Margaret. It is through these meetings that we get a really good sense of what skills and abilities the volunteer candidate possesses and what their motivation is to volunteer. We love to find out what they would like to get out of it!

The most common reasons for volunteering are social contact, work experience, learning or improving English, and to give something back to the local community. Together, the volunteer and the coordinators choose the right role for the person: Staff Support,

Resident Companionship, Elder Support, or Community Support. We also have Volunteer Team Leaders.

There is lots of opportunity for our volunteers to move around engaging in new roles after they've been a part of our community for a while. We also have lots of community groups who come in and do performances, arts, and crafts in groups and those are counted outside of our volunteer numbers of 700-800 per month.

The next step for the volunteer candidate is to attend a group orientation. These are generally two hours long and offered every fortnight. The volunteer coordinators cover everything from the Eden Alternative, information about volunteer roles, health and safety to communications. Volunteers fill our registration forms and are ready to get started for their first shifts—but they are expected to come to another two-hour training session within their first month, to be considered fully registered.

On their first day, a volunteer will be paired up with another individual, or a group, depending on which shift they have chosen or been assigned. We have excellent processes in place for the first few shifts for all volunteers, to ensure we are truly training them 'how to think' and 'how to respond' on their own—so that volunteers do not need to be supervised forever by staff. The idea is to empower them to spend time directly with residents without being micromanaged but given enough support and confidence to do so up front.

Each month there are alternative options for training sessions, the volunteer chooses which area where they feel they need the most support. They are more than welcome to come to any or all of the sessions, but there is a minimum requirement that they attend one more after their orientation. The types of training choices include Eden Alternative workshops, Communication training, Forgetfulness (Dementia) training, Grief training, and Health and Safety training.

We also run a seven-part workshops series, the Knox Practical Communication Course—for volunteers who have English as a Second Language. It's been designed by The Literacy Professionals/Languages International and learners receive a certificate upon completing the training. This is all free of charge as our way to give back to volunteers, as we are a diverse community (63 nationalities and counting!)

Paul: Would you consider your volunteers a reliable resource?

Jill: Ah! Utterly! We got the usual push back when we decided to go down the path of growing a volunteer program. But let me give you just a little bit of my background. Before I came to Knox, eight years ago, I was the CEO of a hospice, and we had about 450 volunteers. We had volunteers giving cares, running our shops and driving vehicles. We had them doing all manner of things. We wanted to keep it really simple here at Knox, to let it develop in its own way with a lot of support.

Paul: As far as the staff, what's the staff attitude towards the volunteer?

Jill: It's wonderful. It probably took about 12 to 18 months until we got a shift in the tone. To start with the staff had to train these volunteers, they felt they were too busy to be overseeing volunteers, it was the beginning. It's all well and good we have volunteers, but we don't know what we'll have in a year. Then it moved to "…we've three or four volunteers in the evening, but we actually need more." And now it's "…we couldn't manage without the volunteers!"

Paul: Would you be willing to say that volunteer programs are well worth the investment?

Jill: That's our motivation too! We won a national award, an Equal Employment Opportunities, (EEO) Trust Diversity award for what we were doing with volunteers to improve the quality of care. We had members of parliament come to visit Knox. We had the Minister for Volunteering come here to celebrate volunteering. We give people every opportunity to speak about volunteering so that they become the voice of volunteering. The best voice of volunteering are the residents and the volunteers. They are a powerful voice.

Paul: That's really all I have; do you want to add anything more?

Jill: Yes, when we started out, we applied for charitable funding. We applied for a grant to employ a volunteer coordinator, and we explained that it would expand our volunteer program. It's a big leap to look for to go out and employ somebody like Kristen who is stopping at Saskatchewan to see another Eden home. We are looking to form a really close relationship and to possibly trade team members with them. We are looking at key partners specifically who might not have the chance to travel outside of New Zealand. Instead, they may have the opportunity to spend two or three weeks working in a totally different care environment.

Paul: That is just awesome! It's very exciting for me to be talking with people, literally all around the world, your energy and the synergy is just wonderful. It also gives me a sense of hope.

It is readily apparent that Jill Woodward has ramped up the volunteer program to become a world-class example of what is possible. Once again, the recurring themes are: 1) starting with a great director of volunteers; 2) including the staff right from the beginning in the planning of the program; 3) creating a stringent vetting process and training program; and 4) providing ongoing volunteer training and growth opportunities for them.

In the Knox Annual Report for 2015-2016[6], the Chairman of the Board of Directors, Dr. Alastair McCormick highlighted the fact that the Minister for Community and Volunteering, the Honorable Jo Goodhew, made a special visit to Knox to see... "the extensive involvement of volunteers at Knox." He also pointed out that the volunteer program was one of the "cornerstones of our Eden Alternative[7] commitment to provide companionship and stimulating activities for Knox residents."

One day I hope I will have the opportunity to see first-hand the Knox volunteer program, but for the moment, I derive great satisfaction in having met and getting to know Jill and Kristen and learning about this vibrant volunteer program.

Baycrest Health Sciences—Toronto, Canada

I saved Baycrest for last. While the programs I've highlighted here are great, the Baycrest volunteer program is, by far, beyond exemplary. In my opinion, it is the gold standard for volunteer programs in nursing homes. So, with that said, it is my extreme pleasure to

---

[6] Knox Annual Report 2015/2016, retrieved from: https://issuu. com/hunter_creative/docs/knox_annual_report_2015-16_web July 17, 2017

[7] More information about the Eden Alternative developed by Dr. William Thomas can be found at http://www.edenalt.org/

report on and highlight what I think might be the world's premier nursing home volunteer program, boasting some 900 adult volunteers and 300 youth volunteers. If you know of a nursing home volunteer program that you believe is better, I would like to hear from you. If you are an advocate for expanding the role of volunteers in nursing homes, you will enjoy reading about this remarkable volunteer program.

During March of 2016, I attended the American Society on Aging conference. I met several like-minded people also advocating for expanding the role of nursing home volunteers. During our conversations, they encouraged me to contact Syrelle Bernstein, then Director of Volunteer Services at Baycrest, in Toronto, Canada.

My first conversations with Syrelle revealed that Baycrest had been training and recruiting volunteers to provide friendly visits, staff support, and administrative support, and had been encouraging the volunteers to create and facilitate their activities for some 20 years. Listening to Syrelle describe the program, it's onboarding process, their training, and the jobs volunteers were doing, piqued my interest to the point that I knew I needed to go to Baycrest and observe the program first-hand. I was not disappointed, in fact, I spent four days repeating the phrase, "This is amazing, just amazing!"

Over the next several months, Syrelle retired and Janis Sternhill stepped into the directorship. I stayed in touch with Syrelle and asked if she would facilitate my visit. She graciously agreed. During the week of June 11, 2017, Syrelle immersed me in the Baycrest culture of care and the Baycrest volunteer program. Having developed the program, she could highlight its salient aspects.

On my first full day in Toronto, Syrelle picked me up at 10 am and we drove to the Baycrest campus. As we drove onto the grounds, the enormity of the operation was striking. We drove by building after building, passed by a huge parking lot, and cruised by the Esther Exton Child Care Centre, and we finally reached the assisted living high-rise. We parked and began to walk towards the Apotex Centre, Jewish Home for the Aged. I remarked to myself, as Syrelle was explaining what was happening in each building, that this campus was not only comprised of all levels of care with a fantastic volunteer program, but it included a research center and had direct ties to the University of Toronto. In my mind, this was the perfect setup.

As we approached the glass doors of the Apotex automatically parted to the left and right, welcoming us into the foyer of the building. Syrelle logged into the VSys volunteer management kiosk mounted on the wall, as she had become a volunteer herself. The VSys tracking system kept a record of the volunteers that were in the building and what they were doing. For the volunteer coordinator, this was great; she could report on volunteer activity in nearly real time and collect critical data on the volunteer program.

Once Syrelle logged in, we passed through another set of glass doors and what I saw took my breath away. Before me, the ceiling burst upward into a large open area, an atrium that extended eight stories upward, culminating in a magnificently skylit ceiling. I was stunned! It was exhilarating! I looked at Syrelle in amazement and asked, "Is this the nursing home?" "Yes," she said with a big smile. It took a few minutes for me to take it all in and to collect myself. Every floor offered the residents the opportunity to look out and around the beautiful, open-air space drenched with natural sunlight, and to the beautiful open area below, where people could gather in this indoor park or garden.

She then gently turned me to the left to see the area where residents, with the help of an army of volunteers, were creating various ceramic pieces and paintings. It was here I met the first in a series of many Baycrest volunteers, each of them wearing the bright blue "Baycrest—Volunteer" lanyard and identification badge. The finished items were on display in large picture windows, facing the interior of the atrium. The paintings and ceramic sculptures were quite colorful and added to the ambience of this beautiful area.

Once I had regained the ability to breathe, we moved on with our tour of the facility. It was unlike anything I had ever seen or even imagined in a long-term care community. As we walked and were greeted repeatedly by volunteers and staff, it soon became very apparent to me that Baycrest not only embraced the concept of person-centered care, but had successfully created a wonderful, authentic, relational culture that was felt from staff to resident, from staff to volunteer, from volunteer to volunteer, and from staff to staff. It was truly amazing.

Syrelle arranged for me to attend several of the activities that volunteers were facilitating or for which they were providing support. Our first stop was a morning session led by a speech pathologist who was aided by several Baycrest volunteers. In this class, the volunteers were encouraging the residents to take part in the exercises, by doing the exercises with the residents and offering some level of comfort and trust for the resident. Often, residents feel more comfortable responding to volunteer requests more readily than staff. Moving on, we attended a comedy hour conceived and led by Baycrest volunteer, Murray. In his early years, Murray was a stand-up comic traveling throughout the United States, bumping shoulders with the likes of Alan King and Billy Crystal to name a few. Today, he was showing clips of his favorite comedians and sharing a few of his original jokes as well. The audience loved it. I am sure that they all received a healthy endorphin boost setting the tone for their upcoming lunch. Murray facilitated this activity weekly.

From there we toured the assisted living area and had lunch with Larry, the Baycrest volunteer I met earlier in the speech pathology session. Among the volunteers I had the pleasure of meeting, Larry represented what I believe Baycrest was looking for in their volunteers, He expressed a high level of commitment, a warm and outgoing personality, possessed the skills to create and/or facilitate activities, had an authentic desire to make a difference in someone's life, understood the significance of what he was doing for the staff and residents, and finally possessed a great sense of humor. There was a lot of smiling and laughing during my time at Baycrest.

I asked Larry how he came to volunteer at Baycrest. He told me that after retiring, he wanted to stay engaged and was seeking out volunteer opportunities. After several unsuccessful tries at various agencies, Syrelle invited him to try Baycrest. That was two plus years before. He admitted, initially, his motivation was not altruistic, but instead he just wanted something to do, something where he could make a difference. Since then he discovered the richness of volunteering and working with older adults. He recounted some of his experiences and talked about how much he learned from the people he came to know. As with many volunteers I have interviewed about their experience, Larry too, talked about how much he was getting from the experience and how good it made him feel. This too is a repeating theme, "I feel like I'm getting so much more than I'm giving."

In meeting with the new Director of Volunteer Services, Janis Sternhill, I was reminded again how critical it was to have a great director of volunteers for creating, growing, and maintaining a sustainable volunteer program. Janis' experience and expert knowledge of volunteer management, research, and her evident passion for both the volunteers and the residents were unmistakable.

As Janis and I talked about the role of the volunteer, she addressed the fact volunteers have the time to sit with a resident, get to know them, their likes, their dislikes, their fears, and their joys. Volunteers get to know someone well enough even to tell if a smile means they are really happy. "And it's not just about the time, but it's also about meeting that honest need to listen to people" (Sternhill, personal interview, June 13, 2017) She continued by saying that the staff was relieved knowing that the resident was relaxed when they went into their room. The resident had a good experience of feeling validated, acknowledged, and feeling like a human being. "We have volunteers that come onto units and staff cheer because they know the residents are going to be happy…and the staff can focus on those needing their attention." (Sternhill, personal interview, June 13, 2017)

I asked Janis if they measured the impact of the volunteer visit; she said the Baycrest researchers had finished two studies. The first two studies focused on the overall engagement of the resident, i.e., how often did they smile, how often did they speak, what were they doing before the volunteer came in, what did they do when the volunteer came in, and what activities were they doing. The researchers also interviewed staff in the same manner, i.e., what was the staff doing before the volunteer arrived, what were they doing during and after the volunteer visit. Feedback from the staff was included as well, i.e., how was their experience with the volunteer, what did they notice on the unit when the volunteers were present, what happened when the volunteers were not on the unit? And in like manner, the volunteers were asked how they felt when they came onto the unit, and whether they felt different when they were with a resident. A third study was in progress to collect data at the individual level.

Janis talked about all the tasks volunteers were doing and assisting with behind the scenes. "A robust training program was developed for volunteers to administer the Client Engagement Survey to residents and hospital patients. This is highly organized with our quality team and the "volunteer led real time client experience surveys" was deemed a Leading Practice by Accreditation Canada in December 2018." (Sternhill, personal communication, March 6, 2019). As I mentioned above, this supported current research that revealed residents were likely to be more open with volunteers, rather than professional staff.

The Baycrest Learning Institute Speaker Series (BLISS) was a new addition to the volunteer program. Professionals from Ryerson University came in and trained people to be facilitators, who in turn trained volunteers to facilitate groups and give presentations. The goal, however, was not the presentation, but engaging the residents in the presentation. Janis offered two examples. The first was a pianist who played a musical piece and then elicited discussion about how the music made the listeners feel and other engaging questions. Similarly, a volunteer from Morocco told her personal story of life growing up in Morocco. "This program was volunteer created, volunteer-run, volunteer trained, and the staff is thrilled" (Sternhill, personal interview, June 13, 2017)

When I asked Janis about liability issues, her response was not surprising, "All of our volunteers are highly trained and starting in January [2017] they have to complete on-line learning modules the same as staff does." We went on to discuss having liability insurance, and there was no "new" news on this topic for me. You evaluate the tasks volunteers will be doing, identify possible vulnerabilities, and then create policies and training to reduce the chance of a mishap.

We discussed the budget and how she justified the volunteer budget. I knew that was an ongoing task. I suggested that one must connect volunteer activity to the bottom line, showing that operations budgets are positively impacted when residents, staff, and families are happy.

Janis pointed out, "We cannot attract young people into gerontology if we don't give them an opportunity to be exposed to caring for older adults. Providing volunteer opportunities provides that exposure. In like manner, what about the thousands of people who are retiring and looking for "something to do?" (Sternhill, personal interview, June 13, 2016)

From there, I brought up the subject of labor unions. Janis said that overall the relationship with the unions was respectful. There were instances when the union leaders wanted some adjustments made to job descriptions or clarification as to what the volunteer job was and that the volunteer was not replacing a paid employee who had just left the organization. The unions wanted to understand what the volunteers were doing. "If we want our volunteers to be healthy and strong, our aging population to be healthy and strong, there has to be strong governmental support to support volunteerism" (Sternhill, personal interview, June 13, 2016).

In meeting with the Volunteer Coordinator, Tehila Tewel, I had the opportunity to discuss their recruiting, onboarding and training processes. It was reassuring to me that Baycrest also had a stringent vetting process and training protocol.

For those of you who follow my articles, you know that I am not only a strong proponent of filtering for highly committed individuals, but also for adequately preparing the volunteers for the roles they will be assuming. As should be clear by now, Baycrest volunteers were embraced by care staff as a valuable and necessary asset not only in providing quality care, but also the quality of life.

Tehila indicated that they hosted orientation/information sessions twice a month, attended by some 50 prospective volunteers at each session. Attendees receive both general and specific information about prospective volunteer roles. Those who apply complete seven modules of on-line training and other screenings and tests, as required by the Ontario Long-Term Care Act. [8]

Screening continues when they come in for their interview with a highly trained interviewer, who is also a volunteer. The interviewer will place them in the program that matches their skills and Baycrest's needs. Many specialized volunteer programs have been created which require more hands-on training and education. Some of these are offered on-line, and others are in classroom settings. Most of the on-line courses and specialized training provide certificates upon completion.

In my own experience with recruiting "super" volunteers, the attrition rate was high upfront, but low on the backend. One thing I have learned in this process is that no matter how desperate one may be for volunteers, simply putting warm bodies in place will not result in an effective or sustainable volunteer program. Filtering for and training highly committed volunteers is a more difficult path but one that will, in the end, produce the kind of volunteer program like the one in place at Baycrest.

---

[8]   The Ontario Long-Term Care Homes Act of 2007, c.8, s.16(1) requires that "Every licensee of a long-term care home shall ensure that there is an organized volunteer program for the home that encourages and supports the participation of volunteers in the lives and activities of residents." And goes on to state: "The volunteer program must include measures to encourage and support the participation of volunteers as may be further provided for in the regulations. 2007, c. 8, s. 16 (2)." Whereas no such statements or requirements exists in the U.S. Nursing Home Reform Act of 1987. The Baycrest Health receives government funding for which the volunteer program receives a portion of that funding. In addition, Baycrest Foundation donors contribute 20% of the Volunteer Services budget.

Without exception, volunteers, wearing the blue "Baycrest— Volunteer" lanyard could be seen everywhere and not just a few. It was so remarkable and refreshing not only to see the incredible number of volunteers, but also that they were truly making a positive impact on the quality of care and quality of life for the people living at Baycrest, as well as the staff of Baycrest.

If you are a director of volunteers or are in the process of establishing a volunteer program in your long-term community, I highly recommend that you take a good look at the Baycrest volunteer program.

I am sure that there are many more exemplary programs. As I continue my journey searching out exemplars, I will continue to highlight them at my blog and other media outlets. Even in the current climate of budget cuts and limited funding, volunteer programs are far more than just a "nice to have if you can afford it." Rather volunteer programs will play an increasingly critical roll in the operations of nursing homes. Otherwise, the people working there will continue to leave the industry, and our loved ones will barely get their basic needs met. There are people in our communities who, given the exposure and subsequent training, can and are willing to roll up their sleeves to help provide both emotional support of the residents and practical support for the staff. It can be done. It is being done. And more leaders need to realize this and pursue developing great volunteer programs for the people who live and work in their long-term care communities.

CHAPTER SEVEN

Re-thinking Volunteers as a Work-Ready Resource

"My greatest challenge has been to change the mindset of people. Mindsets play strange tricks on us. We see things the way our minds have instructed our eyes to see."

—**MUHAMMAD YUNUS**

CHANGING THE WAY people think about anything is not an easy task. In fact, it may be nearly impossible. In reality, I cannot change the way you think. You may not have much luck changing my viewpoint either, however, we can present supporting evidence, such as case studies, empirical data, and real-life examples to each other. In the end, the choice to see and understand something in a new light rests with each of us. It is our choice. Do we stick with what we know or what we think we know? Or instead, do we consider the evidence, take what seems to be a risk and opt for choosing a new path? Changing what we believe about something, in this case the way we view and use volunteers in our nursing homes, may seem like a risky business.

Embracing and adopting a new perspective, a new paradigm, moves us away from that comfortable place of certainty. One's sense of security feels threatened. To help you see what I mean, let me digress for a moment. As I explained in Chapter One, my first exposure to a nursing home was the result of my decision to help keep the music program alive at my church. Answering the pastor's call for help led me to a "new land," a place that I had never even considered or dreamed of going. I am sure that many people could tell similar stories about moving from a place of the known to a place of the unknown only to find a new world of unpredictable but positive outcomes. The difference here is that there are nursing homes already training and using volunteers in expanded roles as you read in Chapter Six. These nursing homes have discovered a rich, work-ready resource.

In the current climate of severe workforce issues; threats to funding; the inaccurate notions that volunteers are unreliable, and create more work for staff and are only capable of the simplest of tasks; the idea of making a serious investment in a volunteer program seems counterintuitive. With this chapter, I describe the characteristics of the "super" volunteers, and I hope you will see that there are people in your communities who are reliable and well worth your investment. My findings are based on my own experiences with the people that came forward to volunteer at Community 360°, as well as the organizations that I highlighted in Chapter Six. In Chapter Eight, you will have the opportunity to meet several of these "super" volunteers. Based on what I am experiencing and observing in many places, I am convinced there are people in our communities who are looking for meaningful volunteer opportunities that offer them the chance to learn new skills. They want to be and can be valuable assets to the professional staff. They want to experience the deep satisfaction that comes from seeing first-hand how they, the volunteers, have made a significant difference in someone's life. If we choose to, we can offer these potential volunteers, the very thing they desire, i.e., to learn new concepts and skills and see first-hand the positive results of their efforts. Moreover, they want to be led by experts; I talk about this in Chapter

Nine. But for now, let me say that they want to be trained and managed by someone who has the training and knowledge to lead volunteers. Creating a sustainable volunteer program is the job for a trained professional. Often volunteer recruiting and management falls to an existing staff person, but for this level of volunteerism, "super" volunteers want "super" leadership. I will talk more about this in Chapter Eight. With this in mind, let us start with the question: "Who are these "super" people that are attracted to volunteering in a nursing home?"

When I started the new training protocol for Community 360° in 2010, I was uncertain who, if anyone, would subject themselves to the intense scrutiny and training we created for volunteers. It was during these initial days of the new onboarding protocol that my incorrect thinking about people was soon corrected! My "uncertainty" was soon mitigated while reading the first application submitted under this new regimen. It was from a United States Air Force pilot. After reviewing her application and having received and reviewed her reference letters, I invited her to meet with me for a face-to-face interview. When she arrived for her appointment, I was stunned. Standing before me was a bright, poised woman, a professional, who, stationed at the Air Force base in Omaha, had, without hesitation, completed the first steps in the volunteer process. Once I gathered myself together, I offered her a chair. She was well-spoken, conversant, answering my questions with clear and thoughtful responses, smiling all the while, and like many of the volunteers we now attract, told me of the great relationships she had with her grandparents and other older adults. Now in the military and stationed far away from family, she felt Community 360° could offer her the opportunity to be with and work with older adults.

As I said previously, her ability to formulate and articulate well-thought-out responses to the interview questions was brilliant and indicated her ability to think on her feet. Being able to think on one's feet is an important quality when working in a long-term care environment. When I brought up the fact that she would have to attend 16 hours of training and pay $50 for the experience[9], she did not even blink. Instead, she agreed, pulled out her checkbook and paid the tuition fee on the spot. Several weeks later, she completed the training. I assigned her to a long-term care community near the base where she was stationed. She volunteered until she received a new duty assignment. I was more than pleasantly surprised and genuinely encouraged to continue with this vetting and training protocol.

Since that first interview, one person after another applied, successfully navigated the vetting process, and completed the training. At the time of writing this book, more than 100 people had completed the volunteer training course.

All our prospective volunteers share similar qualities, i.e., midlife to nearing or in retirement professionals, successful in their careers, poised, articulate, passionate about older adults, and committed, self-starters with the intellectual capacity and desire to learn new skills. Because they have had previous positive relationships with older adults, they are now looking to rekindle those relationships through the people they hope to meet in nursing homes. They want to be trained, and they want on-going training as well. The volunteer's desire for professional training and on-going training repeatedly appears in the research literature (see van der Ploeg et al., 2012).

Armed with my own experiences, plus discovering volunteer programs like those at Baycrest Health Sciences, I am confident stating that people such as these are in your city, town, or village. They are a unique group who, in addition to the qualities I men-

---

[9] The $50 training fee simply covers the cost of the manuals and training materials. It also is a screening device for testing for commitment.

tioned above, share five common characteristics: Compassion; Community; Selflessness; Presence; and Commitment.

Compassion

Some of you reading Compassion may have also read other books by theologian, author, speaker, Henri J. M. Nouwen. If not, I highly recommend any of his books to you. After several years of teaching, Nouwen left academia to work among the mentally and physically disabled at L'Arche in Ontario, Canada, and there he stayed until his death in 1996. During his time at L'Arche, Nouwen wrote what I call, "sticks of dynamite," meaning books that were not painfully long, but were rather succinct works that presented deeply profound concepts regarding serving people who need help. Among those "sticks of dynamite" is his book, *Compassion* (1983), written with Donald McNeill, and Douglas Morrison, both priests and colleagues of Nouwen.

Nouwen (1983, p. 6) introduces the concept of compassion by explaining that much of our living is driven by competition. We aspire to accumulate education, stature in society, job promotions, material goods, wealth and so on with very little of our lives being driven by compassion. Compassion does not present an attractive alternative. Compassion per Nouwen, "asks us to go where it hurts, to enter into places of pain, to share in brokenness, fear, confusion, and anguish" (1983, p. 3). The word itself means "to suffer with." The key word in that phrase is "with." The "super" volunteer fully understands and embraces this concept.

When we go to a long-term care community, we are not going there to "fix," "change," or "convert," someone. The people living in nursing homes are not our "target" population. Rather we have come to be "with" them, to understand their experience, to feel what they feel, to become a fellow sojourner and to become their student. For it is in the nursing home that the volunteer learns what it is to live with the fear of losing one's dignity, one's value, or one's identity, having no sense of security or connectedness to others. It is here, in the nursing home, that volunteers come to realize that they may not know what will happen tomorrow, but that they are here to talk with and to walk with and to remain with someone throughout their journey. During our training sessions, I love presenting the concept of compassion to new volunteers because it frees them from their concerns and their fears of not knowing the right thing to say or the right thing to do. Compassion releases them from a performance-oriented set of expectations, i.e., worrying about what they should say or do. I announce to the new volunteers, "I have good news for you! You do not have to *say* anything, and you do not have to *do* anything. You only need to *be* there." Almost without exception when I announce this, I hear a sigh of relief from the volunteer trainees and I interpret it as their feeling of freedom from restraints on their responses. I think we are all very aware of how task-oriented our society is. We are oriented towards "doing" to the point that we fill every moment of our lives with activity. But why?

When do we take time to stop, to reflect on the day, and to consider the days of our lives? Here in the nursing home, of all places, the volunteers learn and become comfortable with those extended periods of silence, of sitting in the day room holding the hand of another person, of exchanging warm and knowing smiles without the pressure of idle chatter. Being "with" someone is fine. And once again, how much effort do we give to filling our calendars, when that is simply a tactic to avoid intimacy (Heller, 2000)? Heller suggests that we are afraid of being rejected by others, afraid that once they come to know us, they will turn us away. Therefore, we do this strange dance of getting close and then pushing away; we fill our calendars with excuses for why we cannot meet with each other. Yet it is through our effort to be compassionate that we learn how to instigate, develop, and nurture meaningful and intimate relationships. These are the relationships that everyone needs, especially people living in long-term care communities. "Super" volunteers have the capacity and ability to embrace compassion as a way of life.

Community

In 1999, through a Proclamation on Aging, The United Nations proclaimed it as the "International Year of the Older Person." When I learned of this, I made calls to local and state officials to learn how they were planning to participate. Upon hearing their plans, I asked if it would be all right if Community 360° would host an event as well. At that time, we were enjoying a great rapport with about 170 long-term care communities in eastern Nebraska and western Iowa. I intended to make sure that the people living in these long-term care communities were recognized as well.

The first "Nebraska Day of the Older Person" was held October 2, 1999. It was quite successful. We produced the event in Lincoln, the capital of Nebraska. We secured a large room on the University of Nebraska at Lincoln, East Campus. Some 100 older adults from nursing homes, care staff, members of the Department of Health and Human Services, as well as other prominent state officials and politicians attended. Retired Governor Frank Morrison was our keynote speaker. He was 94 years of age at the time and had served as governor of Nebraska from 1961 to 1967. He was well over six feet tall, a commanding presence and key figure in Nebraska state politics. He was quite articulate. I had the current governor, at that time, Mike Johanns, sign a proclamation at the Capitol State Building, declaring the day as "Nebraska Day of the Older Person," which we then presented at the luncheon that followed the signing.

The program included a wonderful lunch, music, and then a speech from Governor Morrison. He started his talk by asking, "Just who are these 'older people?'" To answer his question, he talked about his impression of who the older people are:

"When I was in first grade, the third graders were the older people. Then when I got to third grade, it was the sixth graders who were old. When I reached middle school, it was the kids in high school who were old and finally when I got to college; it was the graduate students who were the old ones. The only thing I can figure out is that the old people are the ones older than me!" (Morrison; keynote speech, 2 October 1999, Day of the Older Person)

Hearing this we all laughed, but that story has stayed with me all these years. The luncheon went over so well that I decided to continue hosting this event for several more years. But it was the "Nebraska Day of the Older Person" event of 2001 that became a defining moment for me and the way I have come to understand the community. Just a few weeks before the event, the World Trade Center towers were attacked. Our event was scheduled to take place on the first Thursday of October. We decided to go ahead with "Nebraska Day of the Older Person" as it represented the community coming together to honor our older adult population.

We secured what was then the Holiday Inn Conference Center in Omaha. We had seating for 500. The Governor of Nebraska, Mike Johanns, attended and brought with him his policy cabinet for the Department of Health and Human Services. Skutt High School sent close to 50 students to help escort the approximately 400 older adults that would be attending. They made sure that our guests made it safely from their vans and buses to their seats in the ballroom. Also attending were several university presidents, clergy representing a variety of religious traditions, Community 360° volunteers and board members, and even a table for a group of former gang members and their adult mentor, a pastor who had taken them under his wing. They were volunteering in a long-term care community in their neighborhood, (That story is a book in and of itself). It was an amazing cacophony of people who would not all normally be in the same room with each other. They represented various religions, races, worldviews, ages, and levels of education. It really was a cross-section of the population, but, for me, the realization, the epiphany moment, came as I looked out across the audience from the stage. I realized the power of older adults to create community.

When it was my turn to come to the podium and welcome everyone, I stopped and just stood there staring out across the audience, scanning the many faces of the people. At that moment, time stood still for me. I do not know how long I stood there speechless at the microphone and thinking, "This is what community is or should be." Sharing this space with me, were people from every background, race, religion, age, and socio-economic status. They were all there, together, enjoying a great meal and engaging in conversation. As a result of that day's event, I came to believe that one of the critical roles of older adults in society is to show us how to create and live in a community. For me, that day was breathtaking, and I have never been the same since.

Sometime after that event, I discovered Jean Vanier, founder of L'Arch, communities. Vanier founded L'Arch to serve the disabled. In his book, *Community and Growth* (1989) he talks extensively about community and how it affects each member of the community. In brief, he explains that community is not formed when everyone comes together and agrees on everything. Instead, community emerges when everyone is being confronted with their ego and needs for attention and the members of the community must choose to stay or to leave. People form community when they decide to remain together, determining that preserving their relationships takes precedence over their agreements and disagreements.

This is not an easy concept to embrace, and it is undoubtedly not easy to do, but it is key to the "super" volunteer. The "super" volunteer must be available to everyone in the nursing home, regardless of what differences may exist between them and the people they serve. The "super" volunteer embraces diversity and the concept of community.

The nursing home is a crosssection of society, and so the "super" volunteer is likely to encounter a variety of worldviews, religious beliefs, generational differences, languages, customs, and even sexual orientations. How is the "super" volunteer to respond to such a group of people? They receive the people living in the nursing home by looking beyond the similarities and differences to see the human being before them who yearns for love and to be loved, yearns for connectedness (Power, 2017a), and yearns for a sense of belonging (Nolan, 2006) (See Chapter Four for a discussion of Power's and Nolan's concepts of well-being and quality of life.)

Our nation, going forward, will only grow more diverse. The "super" volunteer is culturally competent, that is, prepared through training, to work with people from various backgrounds, cultures, races, sexual orientations, and so on. The excellent news is that there are people in our communities who are willing to embrace all people who cross their path. This means they can create a community within your nursing home while becoming a bridge to the outside world, to the community beyond your nursing home walls. They become the ambassadors of your nursing home, coming into your community to bring news from the outside world and then returning to the outside community, bringing with them their stories and news from the "inside" community. How often do we hear the "good news" of what is happening in our nursing homes? The answer is, not often. Instead, we only hear about nursing homes when something has gone wrong. "Super" volunteers bring good news to both your community and the community at large. I tell people that there is a library just down the street with living books; to my friends in the nursing home, I say I have come to think I may need them more than they need me. I need to hear their stories and their wisdom. I need them to teach me the meaning of community.

Selflessness

Tightly coupled with the value of community is selflessness. When confronted with new worldviews, customs, cultures, rituals, and ethnicities, we discover to what degree we are selfless. "Super" volunteers do not wait to see if they can help or be of assistance.

An opportunity to witness selfless people in action is during times of crisis. Of course, no one wishes for a disaster, but in the year 2008, a straight-line wind roared through downtown Omaha with wind speeds reaching about 115 miles per hour. Our offices at that time were in the St. Joseph Tower Assisted Living Community. On that day, June 27, 2008, we were sponsoring a resident and family picnic along with the staff of St. Joseph Tower. There were some 100 older adults with their family and friends scattered across the front lawn. Most of them were seated at portable round tables. In addition to various tents, food carts, inflatable bouncy houses, there was a large stage on which a local band was providing the music. Everyone was having a fun time until the weather alert radio began announcing warnings of an approaching storm with wind speeds more than 100 miles per hour. We had about thirty minutes to react.

It was controlled chaos as everyone worked very quickly to get the older adults inside the tower, secure the tents and tear down the band equipment. With every passing moment, the skies grew darker, and then a large and heavy wall cloud appeared. It looked like something out of a science fiction movie and it was coming straight for us. Everyone was running to and from the front lawn as the massive storm cloud was barreling towards us. Everyone was barely able to get into the building safely, and most of the tents were folded, except one.

When the storm did arrive, with a tremendous crashing sound, it launched the tent straight up into the air and then bent it into a knot. The wind twisted large cottonwood trees like matchsticks, debris was flying everywhere. The wind picked up our dumpster and threw it across the street into someone's car. Large sections of the building on the side being hit by the brunt of the wind were ripped away exposing the elevator shafts. Sitting inside the building, we could hear the roaring wind sounding as if fighter jets were flying at ground level all around us. Then, as quickly as the winds came, they were gone. The silence was startling.

We waited for a few more minutes, listening for clues as to whether the storm had indeed passed. Slowly and cautiously, we ventured outside to view the damage. Our front lawn and our picnic now looked like a war zone. Amazingly though, the eight-foot table with the water balloons, sitting in between the now twisted trunks of the large cottonwood trees, was untouched. Slowly, we began to pick up what remained of our picnic. Then within minutes, men began arriving with tools and chainsaws. I did not recognize them. I assumed that these were people were coming from the surrounding neighborhoods. As if they had received some instructions detailing what their role was to be, they began cleaning up the debris, sawing the fallen tree limbs with chainsaws, picking up trash, and folding and stacking the tables and chairs.

Once things seemed to be under control, I went to my home, which was only a few blocks away, anticipating the worst. When I arrived at my house, I could see that pieces of my roof were missing, the leaves had been stripped off the trees and were plastered to my house. The large trees that lined our street were broken down or had large branches hanging down dangerously close to breaking away from the tree. Again, I was surprised by the reactions of the people. My neighbor had brought a very large forklift from a construction site where he was working and was greeting me as he drove down our street. Accompanying him and standing on one of the extended tines of the forklift, was another of my neighbors wielding a chainsaw. I just stood there with my jaw open hoping he would not fall. He was at least ten or more feet in the air, removing the dangling, and broken tree limbs with the chain saw. Our neighborhood was cleaned up, the wood was stacked, and the trash was picked up in less than two days. Not being very handy with tools, I felt like I needed to help in some way, so I helped by stacking the cut wood. Again, I was awed by the level of cooperation of our neighbors. Selflessness is letting the concerns and needs of others take precedence over our own needs. "Super" volunteers are selfless.

Bill is another example of a "super" volunteer who embraces the value of selflessness. I received a telephone call from a woman in Kansas City, asking me if we had a volunteer in Omaha that would be willing to visit her father who was now living in an Omaha nursing home. I told her I could not make any promises, but I would put out a notice to our volunteers asking if anyone would be willing to make that visit. In the meantime, I thought of Bill, one of our "super" volunteers. I called Bill and talked with him about this need. It turned out that the woman's father liked to play cards. Bill's particular faith tradition frowned on card playing, so Bill did not know how to, nor want to play cards. Then I told Bill that the father was Jewish and living in the Jewish nursing home. Bill was an Evangelical Pentecostal. I do not know if you could find two people further apart in worldviews and religion. But Bill said he would try it once. Three years later, the two men were best of friends, played cards every week and were together when the father passed away. Bill's selflessness opened the door for these two men, these two worlds to come together. His selflessness gave the father the joy of relationship, of feeling connected to someone, and a few hours of laughter. During those years, I was in contact with Bill and asked him how things were going. He would tell me, "Everything is going great! I go to the nursing home to visit and get severely beaten at cards! And he enjoys beating me!" For the daughter, it was a great relief to know that someone was there for her father. Selflessness opens unexpected relationships. Super volunteers understand and embrace this principle.

Selflessness, however, does need to be tempered with selfishness. That may sound a bit odd after those two stories. When the clean-up began in my neighborhood after the storm, I never even considered going up into the air some twenty feet on the tip of a narrow tine of a forklift, armed with a chainsaw; nope, not going to do that. I could only imagine cutting off my hand or arm and then plummeting twenty feet to the ground with the chainsaw following close behind. I was not selfless, but instead, I was selfish; that is selflessness tempered with wisdom.

I bring this up because there is a boundary. I talk to our volunteers about this. My admonition to them is, while they have a profound sense of loyalty and love for the person(s) whom they visit, they must take care of themselves. Otherwise, they will reach a point where they are exhausted and are no longer useful. "Super" volunteers understand this principle. While we do everything we can to bring joy and meaning to the people living in nursing homes, we cannot do it to our detriment. My experience has been developing and nurturing these wonderful authentic relationships with the people I visit, knowing they understand and respect those times when I must say, "I'm sorry, I just cannot do that for you." They know I have their best interests at heart; they know I genuinely care about them; and they know if I can find some way to fulfill their request I will.

Presence

"Super" volunteers understand what it means to be "present." To illustrate this, I will share a story about my son's best friend, Matt.

My son and Matt were the best of friends during their high school years. Both were pretty good skaters able to perform complicated maneuvers such as sliding down handrails, skidding along curbs, and jumping over concrete benches in parks. They spent many hours together. One weekend, during this time, Matt invited my son to go along with him on a weekend fishing trip. It would be Matt, my son, and two more of their friends. My son declined the invitation, as he had other plans for that weekend. Matt and his three friends went on the trip. On the return home, a very sunny early Sunday morning, the boys were riding in a small car traveling east, staring into the sun's glare, causing the driver to miss a stop sign at an intersection. While racing through the intersection, a large conversion van broadsided them. Three boys died instantly at the scene while Matt lived for another twenty hours. Family members, students, and friends filled the hospital ICU waiting room. I remember that twenty hours fairly well, even more than 25 years later. I do not remember so much what people said during that time, but I do remember many of the faces of the people that were there with us, who were present with us.

Going into the nursing home and seeing the people living with conditions such as crippling arthritis, dementia, the ravages of diabetes, paralysis brought on by strokes, I feel helpless. What can I really do for them? We can play games. We can go for walks or wheelchair rides. We can watch a movie or a football game. We can sing songs or maybe make a batch of cookies. But what is it that really counts for them? What is it that really makes the difference for them? The games? Maybe. The song singing? Maybe. But what about those times when we just sit and hold hands in silence? Does that make a difference? Yes, it does. They may not remember what we talked about from a previous visit, but they will remember that I was there. I was present. Super volunteers understand the concept of being present.

During our training sessions, we talk about being present, and what that means for the people they will visit. The headline for those sessions is: "You need not to worry about what to say or what to do, just be there." They may go to the dayroom, or the activity room, find a chair and sit. They may wait, not too long, and one of the people living there will approach you and ask, "Why are you here?" And then the conversation begins. It is hard for us, being task-oriented creatures who live and die by our "to do" lists and calendars. We have schedules to maintain and jobs to do. So, sitting in silence with someone, somehow, does not squelch that drive that we have to be "doing" something. For many of us, it feels very uncomfortable. For me, even after all these years, I still feel the twinge of "…you need to be doing something." It is deeply ingrained in all of us.

The people living in your communities may not remember what you have said from week to week, but they will remember you came to visit them. They will not forget their volunteer's face, their smile, their voice, and even their footsteps. I have one more story to share.

Chuck retired early from a successful career. He was driving a school bus in the morning and afternoon as a way to give back to the community and to have something to do. During one of our many cups of coffee, we were talking about his new job; I encouraged him to use some of his free time to make visits to a nursing home. I contacted an activities director at a home where I thought he would be a good fit and, of course, she was thrilled to have him come in for an interview and to get him started. Chuck eventually became and remained a chaplain at that nursing home for eight years. One day, while Chuck and I were having our coffee, I asked him how things were going at the nursing home. He relayed this story to me:

"I walk the halls of the nursing home and stop in to visit with people. I want to make sure that everyone gets a little visit from me. Last week, I realized, as I was walking the halls, I had missed stopping by to visit one of the residents. I went into her room and began apologizing for not stopping in to visit. She said this to me, 'Chuck, don't worry about it. I can hear you walking the hallways, and that's enough for me. I know your footsteps.'"

I try to imagine a time in my life when, one day, hearing someone's footsteps will be enough for me. Being present for someone is the most precious gift we can offer. Our presence speaks louder than our words and our games. Often, people living in nursing homes will ask me, "Why are you here?" I interpret their question this way: "I know where I am, and I know you could be anywhere but in this place. Why of all places you could be, why are you here?" My response is usually along the lines of "Because I had some time and I wanted to spend it with you." Presence ascribes dignity, value, connectedness, meaning, and love to a person who may be feeling degraded, devalued, disconnected, meaningless, and unlovely. "Super" volunteers understand this concept. Imagine having six of these "super" volunteers on your staff, walking the halls, while the residents listen for the footsteps.

Commitment

Commitment is the foundation upon which the previous four attributes rest. For it is their high level of commitment to serving the people that live and work in nursing homes that gives the "super" volunteer the drive, the tenacity, and the perseverance not only to continue in their role, but also to grow in that role. I found that the Felfe et al. (2008, p. 82) definition most aptly expresses commitment in the context of the "super" volunteer, "...a stabilizing and obliging force that gives direction to behavior and binds a person to a course of action..." The keys words in this definition, i.e., stabilizing, obliging, force, direction, and binds, speak to the needs of the people living in your nursing home. Super volunteers become a stabilizing factor in a world where turnover is so high. Your residents will not make emotional investments in people who may disappear in a month or two, but they will make that investment in a super volunteer that has, over time, proved their commitment. Community 360° has had volunteers in some nursing homes for 15 or more years. Administrators, directors of nursing, nurses, direct care workers have all come and gone, but the Community 360° volunteers have been there through it all. They are a stabilizing factor.

This high level of commitment (along with professional leadership) paves the way for the development of a volunteer program that is sustainable; it is comprised of volunteers who are effective, dependable, self-motivated, and compelled to serve in the long-term care setting. The volunteer recruiting slogan, "You can make a difference," appears on nearly every nonprofit organization's literature and social media. "Super" volunteers, because of their high level of commitment, genuinely want to and do make a genuine difference. It is better to have a volunteer program made up of people who know what the need is, how to meet that need, and have the determination not to stop until they have met that need.

"Super" volunteers will show up on time, every time. They are willing to take on whatever tasks are at hand while respectfully suggesting innovative ideas for programs and activities. They will be proactive in learning what your needs are and how they might be able to help meet those needs. They are team players committed to the success of your community and the welfare of the people for whom you care. They are respectful of authority and your chain of command.

As I mentioned earlier, when I first instituted the new screening and training protocol at Community 360°, I was concerned that people would turn away when they saw what I was requiring of them. But through this experience I have learned when you set the bar high, you will find people who can jump that high. The key is not to compromise your standards. Everyone in this profession is desperate for paid and unpaid help, but merely throwing warm bodies into the mix only creates more problems.

In the case of volunteer programs, there are several types. Some volunteers are "walk-ins." They come in off the street looking for something to do. They may be with you only a few times. Some entertainers come periodically to lift the spirits of the people, like volunteers who come for holidays and special occasions. Board members may be volunteers as well, along with auxiliaries. All of them are important. But what I am proposing is one more layer of volunteers, i.e., the "super" volunteer who, as I have described, brings consistency and sustainability to your volunteer program. Then you can depend on those volunteers for meaningful support, both for the people whom you care for and for the people you employ. Now that I've presented the attributes of a "super" volunteer, let's talk about what they can do.

Expanding the role of volunteers

In addition to providing friendly visits and companionship for the people living in your community, where else could volunteers plug in and offer a helping hand? Would a volunteer be able to help someone get dressed? Would the volunteer be able to help with some personal cares? (Toileting is off limits). Would a volunteer be able to help with physical therapy or speech therapy? What about meals? Would a volunteer be able to assist in the kitchen or the dining area? Could super volunteers be trained to feed people who needed assistance at mealtime? What about administration? Could you plug in a volunteer(s) to help with filing, data entry, collecting and analyzing data? Could super volunteers be used to develop individualized activities for your residents?

You are likely already using volunteers to lead activities. What about using volunteers who would help you create meaningful, individualized activities? One of the emerging themes from my own and others' research is that the people living in your community prefer meaningful and personalized activities rather than large group activities. Super volunteers are trained to listen for insights into "what matters" to the individual. From those insights they can create activities that are meaningful for that person. What about volunteers learning the skills that will allow them to open the doors of communications with people experiencing aphasia? Where else could a volunteer help you and your staff? Maintenance? Transportation? The answer to all the above is "Yes, all of the above," and more.

Remember we are talking about volunteers who have been thoroughly screened, interviewed, and thoroughly trained. They are a cohort of people who are very capable, desire to learn new skills, and want to be a valuable asset to you, and the people living and working in your community. The exemplary volunteer programs that I highlighted in Chapter Six uses its volunteers in many of these ways, but they do not replace paid staff. They augment paid staff, they support paid staff, they may lift some of the workload off paid staff, but I want to be very clear that I am not promoting replacing paid staff with volunteers. You may find that your robust volunteer program becomes a conduit for attracting paid staff!

Now that I presented the attributes of a "super" volunteer let's meet a few of them.

CHAPTER EIGHT

Meet Three 'Super' Volunteers

"I think a hero is any person really intent on making this a better place for all people."

—MAYA ANGELOU

I LOOKED FORWARD TO writing this chapter for some time. When I first implemented the screening process and training curriculum for Community 360°, I was not sure that anyone would want to go through such a stringent onboarding process, i.e., application, reference letters, background checks, face-to-face interviews, and then sixteen hours of training paid for by the volunteer candidate! To my great surprise, relief, and satisfaction, my first "super" volunteer turned out to be an Air Force pilot, stationed in Omaha and then looking for a way to give back to the community. I was stunned. She completed each part of the onboarding process without hesitation and went on to volunteer at a nursing home. From that day forward, it was one pleasant surprise after another. One by one, amazing people would complete the process. One of my great pleasures was getting to the face-to-face interview and waiting for the volunteer applicant to arrive. Who were they? What gifts and talents are they bringing with them? With possibly one or two exceptions in eight years, I was never disappointed.

Listening to their responses during the interview, which would last about ninety minutes, I was so impressed with their depth of empathy for older adults, their desire to serve them, and their willingness to do whatever was needed and to go wherever they were needed. Seeing people of this caliber, day after day, coming to serve, was a clear sign to me that there are people in our communities who are brilliant and capable of providing the meaningful support so badly needed in our long-term care communities. They are self-starters, highly motivated, committed, and have the ability and desire to learn new skills. This is why I began calling them "super" volunteers.

In this chapter, I want you to meet several of them so that you can see for yourself just how remarkable they are and let me emphasize that I believe there are people like these in every town in America and frankly wherever there are people. We have to give them the opportunity and training to serve. With that said, let me introduce you to Joy Rich.

Joy Rich

Joy Rich is one of the warmest people you will ever meet. Her demeanor is inviting, and from the moment you meet her, you know she is someone with whom you want to spend time and that her sensitivity and creativity opened the doors for her to create this program which was recognized nationally by Points of Light. Following are excerpts from my two-hour interview with her:

> **Paul:** Joy, it is a pleasure for me to get to spend some time with you. What led you to want to become a volunteer in a nursing home?
>
> **Joy:** I started my degree when I was 35 years old, and my first class was World Religions, and it really opened my eyes

and how I looked at the world and different worldviews. It made me reflect on what I believe. "Do I believe in a God?" "How am I living my life?" "Do I live the Golden Rule?" "How can you say Christianity is the only religion?" [Taking this course] gave me more empathy?

Paul: The idea of empathy is key; it was like an awakening for you.

Joy: It made me look at the Golden Rule a lot closer. All of the different world religions have a version of the Golden Rule. I decided that was how I wanted to live my life. If I live by the Golden Rule, I'll be ok. I have to put myself in other people's shoes, and be kind, and careful with my words, and seeing the world through other people's eyes.

My dad died when I was seven, and my mother died in 2011. She had four children but never remarried. She was my mom and my "dad." Losing her made me really think about my life. I was watching too much television. I needed to find a way to help people. I told a friend that I was going to volunteer, and my friend said, "You love the elderly. Do something with them." I said, "That's a great idea!"

Paul: What do you think the basis of that is?

Joy: (without hesitating) My great grandma! My mother's mother. My great-grandmother lived with us when I was growing up. She was very important to our family. My mother would not have made it without my great-grandmother. She would garden and provide food for her family. My mother used to say that people would tell her that my great-grandmother was an angel walking on Earth. I would sit with her, and her skin was so thin that I could see her veins. I would pet her hands and follow her veins with my fingers. She gave me so much love. It shaped the way I see older adults.

Paul: So, you went through the training and then were assigned to a nursing home. What was the first day like?

Joy: I remember walking out to my car and sitting in my car crying. People looked like they were overworked and underserved. It was not what I was used to seeing. But I thought, "No, you want to do this. You just have to trust that this is where you are supposed to be." The first day was a little rocky. There was no one there to hold my hand, so I had to just figure it out. It is amazing when you stop looking at the surroundings, and you start looking at the people you start seeing a blessing. I saw what my relationship could be with them. I thought of the things I like to do, so I started a coloring group. At first, it wasn't a big hit as only a few people would come. But one day, the staff brought Bill[10] to the group. He was a bit of a challenge as he talked constantly and repeated himself again and again. But one day, while at the table coloring with us, he said something about a song. I had just bought a smartphone. So, I said, "Bill, let me see if I can play that song." I played it, and then everybody in the group had a song they wanted to hear! So, the next time I came, they asked, "Can we listen to some music?" So now when I get there, Bill is sitting right at the door and he asks, "Miss Rich, did you bring special entertainment?" And now, he has become the "soul" of that group, and everybody in that group loves him, and in the two hours that I am there, he does not repeat himself like he used to.

---

[10]   Bill is a pseudonym.

Paul: You have really seen a transformation.

Joy: Totally! And when he is not there, everyone is sad. One day, though, Bill was not sitting at the door waiting for me. And I wondered why. When I asked the staff about Bill, they told me he could not come to the group today because he was having some behavioral problems. So, I gathered up the others to come to the group. In the meantime, I saw one of the nurses that knew me from the coloring group, and I mentioned to her that Bill could not come to the group. She asked, "Do you think you could handle him?" I said, "Yes! He is the happiest when he is singing and coloring." So, I took him to the group, and there were no problems, in fact, he was singing, smiling, and laughing! I learned later that music was very important in Bill's home as he was growing up. I soon realized he was like a walking encyclopedia for music, titles, composers, their history and so on. He would be great on "Name that Tune."

Once when I couldn't go because I had hurt my back, I called the nursing home to let the staff know that I could not come that week. To my amazement, the group gathered anyway, and one of the staff members brought a tape recorder and so even though I was not there they sang and colored. This really touched my heart that they see this as a family now too. Another resident that has been amazing is Susan.[11] Susan has very limited speech and little or recall, but she is learning the words to the songs we sing, and she is singing. I spoke to a doctor about this, and he let me know that speech and song are generated in different parts of the brain. He encouraged me to continue working with

[11] Pseudonym

her as this was building new neural pathways. So, I'm really careful to make sure that I'm animated, and she is learning the songs. It's just, it's just amazing.

(Joy cont'd) We lose people; they pass away. The hardest one for us was Nancy.[12] She was the first one to pass away from our group. She was loved by all of us. So, I just put a chair at the table and I said, "Buddhists believe it takes 50 days for the soul to travel, so I think she is still here, so, we're going to invite Nancy to sit here, and we're going to go around the table and tell Nancy what we would want her to know and what we liked about her. And so, we all took turns talking to the chair, telling her what we liked about her. Then I said, "Now, I'm going to tell you what Nancy is whispering in my ear and what she would want you to know. Then I went around the table saying things that were unique to each person, one was the best "colorer," another was teased for always saying that he wanted to run off to Vegas with her. Then after, I told each member of the group what Nancy had told me to tell them, I asked the group, "What do you think she is going to do when she gets to Heaven?" They were thinking, and I suggested that she might be dancing. One of the men in the group asked, "Naked?" So, then we had to talk about whether you wear clothes in Heaven (laughs).

It's been life-changing for me. I am so grateful to have them in my life because they have taught me so much about people of different ethnicities, cultures, and worldviews.

------

[12] Pseudonym

Paul: Do you feel like you're a better person?

Joy: Totally better person. I think my empathy has grown by leaps and bounds. I just love going. I just love going there and seeing their smiles and their singing, like Bill. I wish you could see him when he's singing. He just radiates. I'll give him a big grin, and he just gives me this big grin back and starts clapping. How often can you give that to somebody by just being there? I'm going to get a little weepy now when I think how easy this is and how it brings such wonderful gifts if you allow it too.

I go every Saturday, and I remember a lot of the things that you taught in that two-day training. The training was so important to me because I remember a lot of the things that you said. You said it's very important to be on schedule, to keep that schedule. And so, I'm always there. A few minutes before 10:00 and I go every single Saturday. And because of that, they trust me, and they know that I care about them.

Paul: You mentioned several things that you have learned, empathy, interacting with different ethnicities and worldviews, as well as your view of the world has changed. Is there anything else you have learned?

Joy: Well, this is going to sound odd. I don't know that I want to live to be 90, but if I do, I believe I now have the tools to help me deal with it. I'm somewhat of an introvert, and I've learned that if I did have to go to a nursing home, I would have to get out there socially and do things. Otherwise, I think I would go downhill very fast. I have learned to listen to people better and to watch them better, like Sam[13], who does not have speech, but I can read him like a book. I can tell by his expressions if he's agitated or happy. I think empathy is a really big thing and that family doesn't have to be blood, because I consider our group to be family. I mean we all feel connected. One of the songs we sing talks about holding hands, and so I reach out to the persons sitting beside me to take their hand and then we are all holding hands, and, at that moment, we feel that connection.

Paul: Do the staff comment about the changes they see in Bill or Nancy or any other members of the group?

Joy: Yes, they recognize that I can handle Bill because when he is with the group, he's completely different. He is laughing and singing. Sally, who has little recall or language, is learning songs and singing them, when before, the staff thought she had no ability to speak, let alone sing. I feel like the staff respects me now, and I am always respectful to them. I always check with them before I bring someone to our group, and they will come to me and ask if they may bring someone new to our group.

Paul: You've become a part of the fabric of that community.

Joy: Yes, that's a good way to put it. I'm woven into their fabric.

Paul: When you saw what we were going to put you through, as far as the screening process and the training, did you have second thoughts?

---

[13] Pseudonym

Joy: Well, when I saw that there were two days of training, I did ask myself if this was a good way to spend time. I'm busy at work. But then I thought, "What's two days in the scope of your life?" Actually, I was very glad to see that you were asking for references. I thought the training was exceptional and the things that I learned still resonate with me.

Paul: Some people look at the training and decide this is not for me. Why did you decide to go through the screening and training process?

Joy: I was motivated and committed to the idea that I was going to volunteer. If I want to get from point A to point C and have to go through point B, then I will go through point B.

Paul: Joy, thank you for taking the time to share your thoughts with me, and you really are a "super" volunteer.

Note: Joy Rich was honored by Points of Light[14] December 1, 2016, for her work at the nursing home.

Sabrina Teles

Now, that you've met Joy, let me introduce you to Sabrina Teles. Sabrina is a volunteer at Baycrest. Sabrina Teles, in addition to being a Baycrest volunteer is a Master of Arts candidate in Recreation and Leisure Studies at the University of Waterloo. She exemplifies that *super* volunteers are not limited to retirees. When Baycrest created

---

[14] Points of Light, founded in 1990, is an international nonprofit, nonpartisan organization headquartered in the United States dedicated to engaging more people and resources in solving serious social problems through voluntary services

the PLEASE© program (Pleasure for Leisure Engagement for Active and Spontaneous Experiences), Sabrina was one of the first volunteers to complete this specialized training. PLEASE© opens the doors for volunteers to implement individualized activities for each of the Baycrest residents. The activities in which people engage must have meaning for them, otherwise they have little or no effect on their sense of well-being. Large group activities most often used by nursing homes are only effective for the people who find meaning in the activity. In addition to the PLEASE© program, Sabrina completed the Supported Conversation for Adults with Aphasia training. Again, *super* volunteers not only want quality training to prepare them for their roles, but they also want ongoing training as well. Following is our conversation:

Paul: How long have you been volunteering at Baycrest?

Sabrina: For almost two years.

Paul: And what are you doing for them? What are your responsibilities?

Sabrina: I am part of the PLEASE© Program.[15] When you came to visit it was in its early stages, but now we are in the second phase of the research portion. I heard about Baycrest the Sociology of Aging course at the University of Toronto and I thought that sounds like a pretty cool place and I wanted to get experience with the geriatric population. I've worked a lot with kids, so I wanted to expand my experience. I went for an orientation at Baycrest and wasn't too sure I wanted to volunteer for them, but when I heard about the PLEASE© program, I thought it sounded like a good fit for me.

---

[15] Programme for Leisure Engagement for Active and Spontaneous Experiences

So, what I do is visit with specific residents, and we do spontaneous activities that they might want to engage in that day. I bring a variety of things, cards, games, puzzles, an iPad and they say, "Hey, let's do this today," and we'll spend twenty to thirty minutes together.

Paul: So how long do you stay in the nursing home?

Sabrina: Typically, I go on Friday mornings from 10 a.m. to noon. That's usually my scheduled shift because I have school and a part-time job. The first phase of the PLEASE© program was more of a group-oriented activity. I would go onto a unit and try to gather as many residents that were available that morning. It was a little difficult in the morning hours as they were still a little sleepy but now the second phase is more individualistic, so I have specific residents to visit during a certain timeframe.

Paul: So how many residents do you visit with while you are at the nursing home?

Sabrina: In the first phase, I would visit up to eight people in one session, but now in the second phase I will visit up to five individuals, giving each one about twenty minutes of time. I go to their room or find them wherever they are.

Paul: So, the idea is to create activities that have meaning for that person. Have any of the residents you visit come up with an activity you had not thought of?

Sabrina: One of the residents, who usually doesn't leave his room, asked me, "Hey, you know what? Can I show you some stuff from when I was younger?" "Sure, why not," I said. So, he began showing me that he graduated with an engineering degree. So, he's showing me his class photo and asked me to guess which one he was in the picture. Basically, he controlled the whole interaction. He was in his element, and whatever came to mind, he just pulled it and showed it to me. That was a pretty cool experience to have.

Paul: So, he created an activity for you to participate in! Tell me how have your perceptions of older adults changed as a result of your volunteering?

Sabrina: Like I said, I have tons of experience with children, and initially I was very hesitant to work with the geriatric population because, as an outsider looking in, I felt they were very depressing and I didn't know if I wanted to be around that every day or even once a week. With children, they are always happy. It's how you picture them as always being playful. You don't think of the elderly population being that way, especially in nursing homes. Instead, you think of them as sick and frail and just people at the end of their life, and I didn't know if I wanted to step into that. So, I thought about it quite a bit, and in the meantime, I got another volunteer position at the same time at the Aphasia Institute.[16] I started there before I started at Baycrest. The population at the Aphasia Institute was a little younger, middle-aged individuals, and I thought, "Ok, this is fine, I think I can handle Baycrest." So, I tried Baycrest, and honestly, I think it's the best thing I could have ever done. I want to pursue a career in geriatrics now. Someone else will work with children, but not many people want to work with the elderly.

---

[16] The Aphasia Institute trains volunteers to work with patients that are experiencing aphasia.

Paul: So, volunteering has really changed your perceptions of older adults and nursing homes.

Sabrina: Oh yeah! Most definitely! Also, my grandparents have had an extremely positive influence in my life from an early age. They helped raise me. Especially my grandmother, who is turning 90 this Friday! She is a role model and mentor for me.

Paul: Let's go back to the training you received at the Aphasia Institute. Were you trained in the "Supported Conversation for Adults with Aphasia" program?[17]

Sabrina: Yes. I was trained in all of that. It was a pretty lengthy training that you had to complete prior to being a volunteer there. And they had a training that they only asked certain people to do, and that was creating a life story. I was trained to do that as well. A lot of the things I learned at the Aphasia Institute I carried into Baycrest as well. Both have helped me prosper in both positions.

Paul: How strongly do you believe in the mission of Baycrest?

---

[17] See Kagan, A., Black, S., Duchan, J., Simmons-Mackie, N., & Square, P. (2001). Training volunteers as conversation partners using "Supported Conversation for Adults with Aphasia" (SCA): A controlled trial. Journal of Speech, Language, and Hearing Research, 44, 624–638.

Sabrina: Very much! I was taught about their mission and their goals, and as an undergrad,[18] I am still volunteering as much as I can, because it makes me feel good and I can see how I am making others feel good as well. So, I don't mind giving up two or three hours a week or more to do that. It makes me feel better about what I do, and it seems like that I could help make a difference. It's what keeps me going.

Paul: How important is it for you to be recognized and rewarded for what you are doing?

Sabrina: I don't think that it's that important. I received an award in the past for an outstanding volunteer position, and it was great, I loved it. My family came, and it was a great experience. But I don't really need that. Being with the residents is very important to me. It ranks right underneath my school obligations. I've missed work for volunteering (laughs).

Paul: Compare volunteering with children versus volunteering with older adults. What are the similarities? What are the differences?

Sabrina: There are a lot more similarities than I thought there would be. At the end of the day, everyone is human no matter how old you are. Everyone has the same outcome of an interaction whether it's playing a game with a child or doing a puzzle or exploring an iPad with someone older. But with the older adult, it is more insightful. I've learned so much about life and about history especially be-

---

[18] Sabrina is now graduated and working on a master's degree in recreation and leisure studies at the University of Waterloo

ing in Baycrest, a very Jewish community. I've learned a lot about the Jewish culture. I feel like it's a more heightened learning experience for myself. But both are equally fun.

Paul: Thinking about the things that you have learned, is there something that was profound? Any life lessons that came through?

Sabrina: Oh, there are tons! Recently, I was with a resident who was living with Alzheimer's disease. She was thinking she still was living at home with her mother and saying, "You know my mom and me keep getting into fights and I just don't understand where she's coming from. But the other day, I thought, 'She's my mom, and I love her. And life is life.'" And then she started giving me all this advice on how to approach an argument with my mom and how she is still thinking about all these little arguments she'd had with her mom and how she could have approached them differently or how she would approach them differently now. And so, I said to myself, "I'm going to tell my mom I'm sorry for not doing the dishes last night." It's the little things that they reveal that are the main thing.

Then watching her go through a traumatic experience when she had a hip replacement, and now it was the other hip that was injured. Seeing her go through that experience and seeing how sometimes it can be that they're a little neglected, especially if there is a language barrier, not a lot of communication. Seeing how she was treated in a hospital setting and then in the rehabilitation setting, it really encouraged me to want to continue volunteering, to continue a career in geriatrics so I can make a difference in those settings and knowing the hardships that come across, I would still continue my volunteer motivation.

Paul: Speaking of motivation, are the things that motivated you to volunteer being satisfied?

Sabrina: Yes! 100 percent! More than 100 percent! In my undergrad degree, I wanted to do speech pathology. I wanted to work with kids. But being at Baycrest, I've learned about other health professions such as rec therapist, occupational therapists, and a physiotherapist and how much of an impact they have on that population, so now those same motivations I had are still the same, but now I'm on a different career path. I don't want to be a speech therapist. I'm on the fence between a rec therapist or an occupational therapist. So, I still have the same motivations, the same goals, just now a different path on how I want to get there.

Paul: That's awesome! This is one of my arguments for volunteer programs, in that they attract new workers. So, six years ago, the idea of working in a place like Baycrest…

Sabrina: Oh my gosh, it frightened me. I had never pictured myself working with elderly individuals. I might be going in not having a good day, but maybe they can make my day better.

Paul: Has that happened?

Sabrina: Yes! 100 percent! One day, when I was a little bit upset, I had recently got back one of my grades, and I wasn't happy with it. I worked really hard and the teacher didn't acknowledge how hard I had worked on it. So, when I went in, I was not very happy, and I voiced it to a resident that I was speaking to. I said, "You know what? I'm not very happy today." She said, "Oh, why? What's the matter?" I said, "You know, I got a bad mark." She said, "You know what? That's ok." And hearing her say that made me feel better even though my mom had told me the same thing that morning. It sounded so different hearing someone that didn't really know me very well and then hearing her tell me that it's just a mark and I'll get over it.

Paul: I've had that same sort of experience. Why is it when an older adult says something like this, it seems to carry more weight than when someone like your mom says it?

Sabrina: You know, I don't know.

Paul: It's an interesting question for sure.

Sabrina: Could it be that they have so much more wisdom? And they all come from very different cultural backgrounds. They can share that insight that maybe my mom was right or whoever told me that was right in the first place.

Paul: So, on a scale from one to seven, to what degree are you concerned for other people? One being the least concerned. Where would you rate yourself?

Sabrina: I would say a six.

Paul: It's apparent that you have learned a lot through your volunteer experience. How has your volunteer role impacted you as a student, as a friend, as a human?

Sabrina: I'll start with the student. So, as a student, it has helped me with time management because I had so many things scheduled for a week to get this assignment done by this day, volunteer this day, and do this on this day. Also, it helped solidify a lot of the things I was learning by the textbook. So, being in a sociology of aging class or being in a linguistics class, learning about speech sounds and then seeing certain things in the nursing home really solidified what I had been learning by texts, was amazing. So, in terms of student, it heightened my learning experience.

Paul: How about the impact it has made on your relationships with other people?

Sabrina: I think I have learned to have a lot more patience working with some elderly individuals especially those who are losing a lot of their communication ability. Learning to be patient and not rushing or speaking for other people is one thing I've definitely learned to not do. Sometimes, my brothers or other family members I attend to, I will speak for them, "Oh no, he doesn't like that," or "Oh, he doesn't like that on his pizza." They could speak for themselves, and I've learned that working with the elderly population, in that they can communicate. They can communicate for themselves. We don't have to do that for them or assume what they are trying to say. I have definitely learned patience and respecting someone's way of communicating.

Paul: So, what would you tell your friends and fellow students about your volunteer experience?

Sabrina: I definitely try to recruit people as much as I can, since I don't know how many people know about the PLEASE© program, to begin with or are really aware of the opportunities that they could do to volunteer. I can't share a lot of personal information with others, but I will say, "You know what? I had a great day. I visited my friend at Baycrest, and we played a card game, and they taught me a new card game. Do you want to try playing later today?" And often the response is, "Yeah, sure why not." So, I've carried a lot of the things that I've learned and try to show people that it can be fun to volunteer. It is not always supposed to be something like, "Oh, I have to go volunteer for my resume." It can be something fun. It can be something you look forward to doing.

Paul: Yes! Another argument that I use is that the volunteer becomes a bridge between two communities. You go in, and your perceptions about the nursing home have changed. So, you go back to your friends and say, "Hey, it's not what I thought it was." When you go to a nursing home, the older person asks, "What's going on out there?" And so, you become this conduit or connector.

Sabrina: Even just asking me about the weather or what month is it today. "What day is it today, what is the weather like?" I feel like, oh, I have all this knowledge I can share with them, and it's amazing, and then a split second later they're sharing knowledge back with me; it's a great transfer of information.

Paul: If I ask you to tell me one of your favorite stories about your volunteer experience, which one would you tell me?

Sabrina: I think I have one I tend to tell most people about. I was interacting with a female resident for the first time, so I read her patient profile. I learned that she was a professional artist and art professor. I assumed she would enjoy engaging in an art activity with me. So, I suggested that we color a picture together with crayons. She got very angry with me, as I just insulted her. I was treating her like a child in that this was a child's art not the art she once did. The nurse came in and had to help me calm the resident. I apologized, "I'm so sorry I didn't know that I did something wrong." I just figured in her profile that she likes art and she did art so I thought that might be a good connection. We waited a few minutes to let the resident cool down. I went back. She, luckily, forgot about our last encounter.

So, I restarted the conversation. I restarted how I approached it. And every week, I would go in and try to talk about art with her, asked her to show me some of the art she used to make or art that she specialized in and that stuff she would teach. "Hey, why don't you teach me how to draw. Or teach me how to shade in that way, or paint in that way?" And eventually she started painting again, and I have one in my room that she painted, specifically for me. It came full circle, going from her yelling and screaming at me that I insulted her and that was something of her past, now something that she does again that she enjoys doing and looks forward to doing. That would probably be my most inspirational experience.

Paul: Is there anything you would like to add?

Sabrina: My experience at Baycrest has been with dementia or Alzheimer's patients, but I have had an opportunity to experience other parts of Baycrest, as well, like going into the hospital wing and seeing other parts of community life at Baycrest and different people with different cognitive impairments. Baycrest is such an amazing place and I hope they can maybe work my way into really working there and I just never want to leave and stay there for as long as I can, even if it is just a volunteer capacity. I think that's enough for me. But [Baycrest is] definitely an amazing place.

Paul: Can you talk about the training you received?

Sabrina: Yeah for sure. So, when I first started, there was a formal orientation process for all volunteers at Baycrest. Then after that, you have an interview process where they try to find something that best suits your interests or flexibility when you are able to come in. So, I had overlooked a bunch of them like hockey night. Saturday hockey night[19], [you] come in and talk about hockey with the residents, watching the Leaf's play or whoever is playing that night. I like hockey, but I don't know if that's something I want to really commit to doing. And they had something called the PLEASE© program. Ok, let's try that. It has a lot of training for this one where a lot of the other ones are just friendly visitors[20]; you don't really need much training aside from the general orientation that you received. I told them I was up for training, that's fine. I was given a rundown of what the goals for the PLEASE© program were. I was trained and learned how to navigate Baycrest. It was very confusing for me, at least, it was at first. And then I got a sit-down training that went through recreational therapy and what it is and the strategies they implement and how we could help them with their goals and their missions.

---

[19]   The hockey night program was the brainchild of a youth volunteer because so many residents were watching alone in their rooms. He wanted to get them all together to share the energy and excitement. Working together with the Therapeutic Recreation team they implemented the program and the volunteer recruited many friends.

[20]   There is training for friendly visitors that is done by the recreation team, but it is not formalized like the PLEASE© training.

Paul: About how long was the training?

Sabrina: All Baycrest volunteers have mandatory orientations and online modules that we need to complete such as a Responsive Behaviors Module, Patient Safety, and Privacy for Volunteers. We also have optional trainings and workshops that we can attend as a part of our extra learning opportunities, for example, storytelling workshops, and feeding workshops etc. Since the PLEASE© program is a part of a research initiative, I had to complete ethics training as well as specific in-person trainings from various recreational therapists. This in-person training was on-going, but we had two formal sessions. One at the start of the first phase of the PLEASE© program and then one again at the start of the second phase. These sessions allowed the volunteers to work alongside the recreation therapists who would show us different materials that we can use, i.e., large iPads, books, cards, games etc., and how we can engage in different types of spontaneous activities with the residents. Throughout the duration of the research phase of the PLEASE© program I would often have debrief meetings with staff and researchers. We would reflect upon things that worked well and things that did not work as well. In general, I would share my experiences and they would take note and let other volunteers know how they can approach similar situations.

How a typical Friday morning would look for me: I would arrive on the unit around 10 am and would go about my daily activities trying to interact with residents, and then once my shift was over around 12/12:30 pm, I would visit the research supervisor. I would often be required to document my visits with certain residents, filling out pre-and post-visit questionnaires where I would take note of their level of alertness, feelings/mood and overall engagement. This was specifically required for the research aspect of the program. However, there was always great communication between volunteers, and staff members on the specific unit and research and other staff members that were a part of the PLEASE© initiative. So, there is a lot of training in terms of evaluations and observations for the research aspect of it [with] ongoing training and learning experiences.

Paul: And you like this?

Sabrina: I like the structure as well having someone to speak to before or after my interactions and getting advice if I need it.

Paul: Thank you for sharing your volunteer experience with me and have a great day!

Sabrina: Thank you! You too!

Lisa Hayes

Lisa Hayes is extraordinary. As the senior instructional designer for her company, she found that volunteering in a nursing home was a way she could exercise the tenets of her faith, i.e., helping those in need. Also, Lisa has years of experience in volunteer management and serving on boards. She compared her volunteer experiences and found that the need for volunteers is greatest in nursing homes.

Paul: Lisa, thank you so much for agreeing to let me interview you for this book. So, let's get started. How long have you been volunteering with Community 360°?

Lisa: Seven and a half years.

Paul: Wow! Did you just say seven and a half years?

Lisa: Can you believe that Paul?

Paul: No, I cannot! When you made the decision to volunteer, was that something you did right away, or did you take some time to think about that?

Lisa: I had to take time to think about it. I made the decision to volunteer quickly, but I took the time to try and determine what organization I wanted to be affiliated with. That took a little bit more time. I had a very logical type of research. That's the way my mind works. I take a long time to think through things. I wanted to make sure that I was affiliating myself with an organization that I felt comfortable with. So, it did take a little bit of research and time on my part.

Paul: What was influencing you, what was driving you to think about volunteering?

Lisa: I don't know if I can really pinpoint a specific point in time or as to things that happened in my life, that gave me the decision to start volunteering because I honestly think that volunteering has really been in my makeup forever. That's the way I was raised. We were taught to volunteer as children. I always did volunteer; even as a student, a high school student, I was volunteering. So, it was just pretty much a way of life for me. And I think that a lot of that is just me, the way that my parents brought me up. So, I don't think I can really highlight a point in time that made that decision for me.

I think it's more just from a lifestyle type approach which is like I said it was the way that I was brought up. I do believe, being a believer, I think that we are called to serve. And so, I think that has a lot to do with it too. Because I see volunteering as serving other people and that's what I wanted to fulfill my faithful walk of life in this world, so I think it's just very innate in my personality the way that I was brought up.

Paul: So how strongly do you believe in the mission of Community 360°?

Lisa: Ok, I have to confess, when I looked at that question last night, I said I don't know what the mission statement is, so I got on the website and I looked at it, and I thought that's a great mission statement. I love that statement. And I especially wrote down here the phrase "…creating opportunities for people to serve." That phrase in the mission statement is what really spoke to me. But again, that kind of goes back to what I just said. I feel like I've been called to serve and so that part of the mission statement I really liked, so I endorse it 100 percent.

Paul: So, I think I know the answer to this next question, but how important is volunteering to you? Is it a matter of being true to yourself or are you in it for the fun or to make friends?

Lisa: Yes. It's pretty much what we talked about before. It is something that's very important for people to do.

Paul: How important is it for you to be recognized or rewarded for your service?

Lisa: Well, let me just answer this way. I volunteered in a professional organization for a great number of years. I was on a national board, and my purpose on that board was to manage volunteers. And during that time, I created this three-legged stool, in my mind, of volunteer management, the three "R's:" recruit, retain, and recognize. Recognize could easily be replaced with rewards, but I just felt like not only were all three of those facets really important, but I do think they're cyclical. I think that if you continue to do that over and over again with your volunteers, because you know after they've been recruited, and you've trained them and retained them and recognized them, well, then you may want to move them into some other type of opportunities where you need to re-recruit them into something different.

But I also think that you know for everyone that recognition piece, that reward piece is going to be variable. I think it's necessary. You have to have that. People have to be acknowledged for what they're doing. Now to the level, so their acknowledged to the level that they're rewarded and recognized is up to each of the volunteers. But you know, I've always felt like if people care enough to give up their personal time to volunteer, then it's important enough to let them know that first, from a business standpoint, how is their performance, i.e., Are you doing well? Are you meeting our expectations? That type of thing, and then also to acknowledge what they're doing so that they feel like, "Oh, great I am adding value. I am doing something that's appropriate." So, I think the reward and recognition pieces are extremely important. It's just that it varies based on the volunteer.

Paul: As far as different roles that you have, you're a spouse, parent, employee, where does the volunteer role fit? Where would you rank that one?

Lisa: That was an interesting question. I thought about that for a long-time last night because I've never really, well, I can't say never, but I haven't thought about ranking those in a long time, but here's my ranking hierarchy I came up with. At the top of the list is being a believer. Second, it's my family roles, so I grouped everything together from spouse, daughter, mother, and grandmother. The third level is a volunteer, and the fourth level is an employee.

Paul: As far as your sense of who you are, how important is that volunteer role?

Lisa: It's extremely important. When anyone ever asks me, what is it that you do for a living, somehow, I always put in there the passion that I have for volunteering, especially in the capacity that I'm volunteering right now. It's really… it's a lot of how I identify my sense of self. It is a very much a part of my sense of self.

Paul: Compared to your other volunteer experiences how does this volunteer experience stack up?

Lisa: Another excellent question. I think that I received the… OK here's a kudos for you Paul. Of my volunteer experiences, I was the most thoroughly equipped and prepared and trained for this one. So that's kudos to you for the training. Other comparison points that I jotted down while I thought about this, is that I feel like this is the greatest need that I'm volunteering for. You know when I volunteered for that professional organization, people, my peers in this industry, they need guidance and mentorship and all of those types of things, but that need is not as great as what I see with the nursing home. It's by far the greatest need.

And the other thing that I thought of last night is that this volunteer role is very self-directed. It's very individual. So, I pretty much go every Thursday night. But it is up to me to do that. It is up to me to determine what I'm going to do with those residents. I pretty much chart my plan of action, and then I do it as I want to do. Like when I used to volunteer at the church and teach Sunday school class, you were always on a team. You always had to work with other volunteers and make sure that there is a certain level of consistency. But it's not that way here; it's very self-directed. For Community 360° volunteers, if you don't have a high level of self-direction and a high level of initiative, I don't think you're going to be as successful as other people could be. Does that make sense?

Paul: Yes! It sure does. And that has been an underlying theme in my mind as to who we want to recruit. You have people that have a high level of commitment and can think on their feet and have the ability to plan and execute that plan.

Lisa: Absolutely!

Paul: Otherwise, I'm spending my day on the phone calling people, "Did you make your visit yesterday?" Or, getting a phone call from the nursing home saying, "Lisa didn't show up again last night."

Lisa: Exactly! You have to have that discipline.

Paul: From the standpoint of the older adult, they have to be able to anticipate that visit.

Lisa: Yes!

Paul: Their authenticity radar is really sharp, isn't it?

Lisa: Oh yes, I agree.

Paul: They know if you are for real. I mean they really know that. What is your highest level of education?

Lisa: I have a two-year college education.

Paul: What keeps you coming back week after week?

Lisa: This was kind of interesting. And I wanted to put it into three different buckets. First thing I thought of was that just by nature I am a really high level of loyalty and commitment to something. So, in any aspect, whether it's work or family, whenever I commit to something, I rarely back down from it. My daughter used to give me a hard time. She would say, "Mom, your sense of loyalty is out of control. If you really don't like that doctor, it's ok to go to a different doctor." (laughs) But you know that's just my style. I have that high sense of loyalty.

I think the second bucket that I thought of, it's just the joy and the satisfaction that I receive from doing this volunteer work. And when I go on Thursday night, I have a pretty taxing job, and by Thursday, mentally, I'm getting pretty wiped by that time. I am the first to admit that there are some times when I'm driving to the nursing home, Thursday night, and think, "Oh my gosh, I think I'd rather be on the couch." I'm getting really tired from the week, but it is just remarkable to me how I just turn a 180 once I'm there, when I'm driving back home, and I always think, I'm so glad I did that because it took me out of myself and it forced me to focus on someone else. And it just gave them such joy and satisfaction. And the third piece of it is the resident's response, their sincere appreciation for what we do. You know if they didn't appreciate me, I would have a hard time having the motivation to continue doing it. You know that appreciation they have is so evident and that keeps me coming back.

Paul: On a scale of one to seven, to what degree are you concerned for others, one being the least?

Lisa: I give myself a six. I would like to give myself a seven, but I get my six.

Paul: What have you learned from this experience?

Lisa: I got a number of bullets here. I've learned a lot. I've learned the current state of the elderly in these United States I had no idea; I absolutely had no idea. I learned the level of care that is given in nursing home communities, much of which makes me very sad, but there's the level of care, it's not at the level that I thought it was. Number three, I have learned the resiliency of the elderly and it is amazing to me that very rarely do I see any resentment in them. And you know I'm thinking, *OK if I had to give up everything that I have my own home and which everything to be in a nursing home I would have a lot of resentment.*

It's true, and I never see that with them, and they're so resilient. The next bullet was the employee transition in the nursing home. I just see a new face, I swear, every week when I'm there; I can't believe the turnover. Number five is the impact of what loneliness can do. But I guess on the reverse side of that is how you can pull someone out of that state. Oh, here's a good one. I just never realized. I was really surprised at the [number of] younger residents that were in nursing homes. You know I always kind of had that picture that you're 80 and above, but there are people that I work with that are my age [living there]. So, I was really surprised to see that.

And then the last thing I jotted down was, I learned the physical condition of the facility which is not good, and you know it's not as clean as I thought it would be. One of the residents came into the room the other night, people were wheeling a wheelchair that only had one arm on it, and he is a stroke victim. The arm that was gone was on the side that he needed the support of his paralyzed arm, and so it's just hanging down off the side of the chair. You know it is just that the physical conditions, it's just in some cases, it's just horrendous.

Paul: In a way, you have already answered this question about how your visits have to nursing homes changed your perception of what they are…

Lisa: Huge! Huge difference. And I do think, Paul, a lot of this comes from my previous exposure to nursing homes when my grandmother was in the nursing home. You know I was raised in a small rural community in Nebraska, graduated with 18 people in my class. The town only had 700 people in it. So, a nursing home in a community like that, where it has full community support, and everyone embraces it, is just completely different than what you see in Omaha, Nebraska. So that was my vision of [the nursing home] it paid for a grandmother to be there. It was nice and clean, with quality of care... it's my next-door neighbor that's taking care of her. It was a lot different than the reality of what I see today.

Paul: Do you believe your motivations for volunteering are being satisfied?

Lisa: Absolutely! Above and beyond!

Paul: This is kind of like the same question but in the reverse direction. Your volunteer experience, how is it? How might it have impacted your role, your faith, your family, you as an employee?

Lisa: I think it definitely has grown my faith. It definitely has grown my faith. I feel like I have identified one of the purposes God had intended for me when He created me. There's a reason why, from the time that I was a little girl, I remember that at family reunions, I always hung out with my aunts and uncles and not my cousins. (laughs). I mean from a very young age I had a passion for the elderly, and I just feel like God has used this experience to help me fulfill a specific purpose that He had for me in my life and that this is the way that I can give back to these people. I think from a family perspective, I think the way that this impacted me and that maybe it's impacted them, is that they admire me for my commitment that I have with this. They've made that comment many times that, "Oh, no we don't play anything on Thursday night. That's sacred. That's Lisa's night to volunteer." So, they're very proud of the commitment that I've placed with that. From a work perspective, I think the way that it impacted me is it helps me, maybe not on the professional side of work, but maybe for just the personal relationships, that you have a lot of really encouraging people to volunteer and helping them understand the value that we will receive from it, because you know life is just not I go to work, and I come home, and that's it. I mean, there's just so much more to life. So just really encouraging people to find out what their passion is and consider volunteering in that area.

Paul: What would you tell your friends and coworkers about your volunteer experience?

Lisa: This was kind of funny when I thought about this question, because I thought, "Oh Lisa, it's just like you're at work and you're building a business case." If you're requesting something and you have to build the business case for it. I thought, "Okay, what if I told people by trying to encourage them to volunteer…what if I tell them about the gratification that you will experience yourself, because of the appreciation you receive from the residents and how you how you can do something, what you feel is so small, yet they just view it so big.

Here's an example. I couldn't believe this happened. Right before Christmas, I made up these little goodie bags, you know, for each of them. It had like a pack of crackers in it, a chocolate bar and you know just these type things. And in each of those bags, I had a Christmas card. And as I passed around and people were opening up their bags, I heard two different people comment on that Christmas card, "Ohhhh…. a Christmas card. I can't wait to put this in my room. Look, Lisa has signed this Christmas card. This is so neat."

And I thought, "Oh my gosh there's this whole sack of candy and treats that they probably never get, but they're going off on the Christmas card. You know." So, it's something, something so little. It's amazing to me you never know how they're going to respond to you. I think I said this, but you know I always tell people, "Look you'll never have a more gratifying and rewarding experience when you kind of get out of yourself." I don't say it that way, but you know what happens when you decide that it's time for me to give back to other people and the residents and this type of volunteering is the best way to do that. Because if you volunteer at a daycare, those little kids can't express their appreciation to you, but with elderly residents, I mean, it's so overflowing, the love that they give back to you. You won't ever experience that in any other type of volunteer capacity.

Paul: So, I was going to ask you about one of your favorite stories. Was that one of your favorites?

Lisa: I do have another favorite story. It was also Christmas time, and it was a different Christmas time. We were having treats, and I asked everyone to go around the table and name one Christmas wish that they would have. And I specifically remember someone asked for jeans. Someone else asked for chocolate candy. There were some that went a little more on the soft side of things like world peace and those sorts of things. So, then it was probably the eighth resident in when it got to his turn. He just looked at me, and he said, "My wish is for you to know how much you mean to us." Oh my gosh, I'm going to cry. I mean it's just that happened a number of years ago, and every time I think about that, Paul, it just brings tears to my eyes again.

If you only knew how much that meant to me that he said that. I mean, that was the one Christmas wish that he had. And that experience, that story, is just forever imprinted on my brain and my heart. I will never forget that.

Paul: Wow! For me, those kinds of experiences, I mean, I don't know what else I'm experiencing as far as trying to make Community 360° work, but that kind of response makes it all worth it.

Lisa: Yeah, it really does. Absolutely. Absolutely. Yeah.

Paul: Thank you very much for this interview.

Lisa: I certainly appreciate you reaching out to me and being interested to hear my feedback. I think that's wonderful. Thanks very much.

Paul: You bet! Have a great rest of your day!

Recurring Themes

In these three interviews, several recurring themes emerged and I'm sure if space permitted, several more of these interviews would have those themes appearing in them, as well. As it turns out, this chapter has become a mini-qualitative study. Following is a list of several of these themes accompanied by some discussion of each.

Positive past relationships with older adults

In each case, the three-people interviewed in this chapter, when asked about their favorite older person, without exception they point to a grandmother, or in Joy's case, a great-grandmother, "She gave me so much love. It shaped the way I see older adults." For Lisa it was her aunts and uncles, "I always hung out with my aunts and uncles and not my cousins." And Sabrina states, "My grand-parents have had an extremely positive influence in my life from an early age. They helped raise me. Especially my grandmother, who is turning 90 this Friday! She is a role model and mentor for me."

After interviewing hundreds of people, who then went on to become "super" volunteers, I found that positive comments about past relationships with older adults are common among them.

A desire to learn about other cultures and to become empathetic towards others

The focus of the "super" volunteer is "others" versus "self." Again, to me, this is a critical attribute to creating a robust volunteer program. The super volunteer comes without an agenda, but rather comes to serve and to learn. Sabrina states: "It makes me feel good and I can see that I am making others feel good as well." Lisa rates her concern for others a six on a scale of one to seven. And finally, Joy, during her comparative religions class, realizes of that there are many worldviews and that her faith allows her to embrace others, including the people she spends time with at the nursing home. She expresses it this way: "I think my empathy has grown by leaps and bounds. I just love going. I just love going there and seeing their smiles…"

Super volunteers are perceptive and creative

In each interview, the volunteer was alert enough to notice and act on the things that mattered to the people they were visiting. In Joy's case, the coloring group became the "Karaoke & Coloring Group" because she recognized how important music was to one of the members of the group and rather than overlooking that resident's interest in music, she incorporated it into the activity. When the resident felt valued, his behavior changed. Through the PLEASE©

program, Sabrina was trained to create individualized activities for the people she visited. "I bring a variety of things, cards, games, puzzles, an iPad and they say "Hey, let's do this today," and we'll spend twenty to thirty minutes together."

Super volunteers are reliable

The super volunteer has a high sense of accountability and commitment to their obligations, which include their commitment to the nursing home and the people who live there. Each of the people interviewed in this chapter state exact days and times they are in the nursing home and each one rarely misses their "appointments."

This level of commitment is critical as gaining the trust of the staff and confidence of the administration in the volunteer program. I have often heard from volunteer managers that they will train people only to have them show up a few times or not show up at all. Screening people for this level of commitment is crucial to the success of the volunteer program.

Super volunteers want more education

In many cases, even as these three interviews show, the super volunteer has an education beyond high school. Joy and Sabrina completed bachelor's degrees, while Lisa completed a two-year college program. While I have never made this a "requirement," I have observed that most people who make it through the volunteer screening and training do have degrees. I think this goes to the fact that they are looking for meaningful volunteer opportunities and they are not turned off by the screening and training requirements; instead they embrace the opportunity to learn new skills. Research also supports this idea (Damianakis et al., 2007; Van der Ploeg et al., 2012)

Conclusion

Our cities, our towns, our neighborhoods are filled with people such as these three people I interviewed. I wish I could have interviewed a dozen more, but these three people are representative of the cohort of volunteers that can be tapped into, if only you will offer them the opportunity. When you see, first hand, the high caliber of people, such as the people I present in this chapter, supporting the residents day-after-day, week-after-week, month-after-month, while hearing the positive feedback from staff, "…we couldn't do what we do, without the volunteers…," and hearing the feedback from the residents themselves, "…they are like family to us…," seeing the declines in incident rate for falls, negative behaviors and use of psychotropic drugs, how can you not conclude that a serious investment in your volunteer program will produce positive dividends for everyone involved? Over the next several decades and some say for the foreseeable future, we will need to provide care for millions of older adults. Facing severe workforce challenges, we cannot afford to ignore any valuable resource, and that includes recruiting, screening, and training "super" volunteers.

CHAPTER NINE

Creating a 'Super' Volun-Cheer Force

―――――

*"The audition/interview is not over yet. When I've decided
this is someone we need and want, I stress the need for
commitment. Being part of the choir is a special opportunity
not to be taken lightly. We expect good attendance, punctuality,
and participation... This is not the place for a person...who
will or will not come if he or she receives a 'better offer.'"*

FROM "CREATING FOUR-PART HARMONY"

by Lois & Fred Bock

I T MAY SEEM a little odd that I would be quoting a book
on developing a church choral program, but as I have discovered repeatedly throughout my days, everything that I've learned
or have experienced through life events comes into play, again and
again. In this case, through this book by the Bocks, I learned that
developing a program starts with setting standards. In the case of
the Bocks, they inherited a choral program that at best would be
described as flimsy, poorly supported by the congregation and con-
tinuously in search of new choral members because of the high
turnover rate. To correct this ongoing revolving door scenario and
to raise the stature of the choral program in the eyes of the con-
gregants, the Bocks instituted new standards, higher expectations

for participation in the program and consequences for not meeting these "new requirements."

To begin, they required all of the members of the choir to audition. Before their arrival, practically anyone that walked through the door could join the choir. Whether they could sing or not was a secondary consideration to filling a seat. I would have trouble estimating how many times, in my conversations with nursing home staff about volunteers, I heard, "The volunteers are not dependable. I train them, I give them some responsibility and then they don't come back." My response goes something like this, "Well, what did you expect. You expected little, and that is what you got." Not everyone that was in the choir was still in the choir after the Bocks conducted the auditions.

Then to add insult to injury, the Bocks put new rules in place. The first being, missing two choir rehearsals would result in automatic dismissal from the choir. This may sound harsh, but before the Bocks' arrival, I would imagine that listening to the choir on Sunday morning was harsh. It seems counterintuitive, but as a result, the revolving door to the choir slowed to a snail's pace. In fact, there was now a waiting list to join the choir. The choir's stature was now elevated in the eyes of the people who wanted to join the choir, as well as in the eyes of the congregation and the leadership. The choir was no longer some slipshod effort but rather an asset to the congregation. The same process is applied here to the volunteer program. You will get what you expect, and if there are no consequences for not meeting standards, the revolving door on your volunteer program will be spinning furiously.

So, the first thing in setting up your volunteer program is to hire a great volunteer manager who understands and has proven experience applying the principles of good volunteer management. When I asked Jill Woodward, CEO, how she was able to develop such a healthy and vibrant volunteer program at Elizabeth Knox

Home and Hospital in Auckland, New Zealand, without hesitation she shot back, "You start by hiring a great director of volunteers!" The volunteer manager, or as I prefer to call them, the director of volunteer engagement, should carry the same stature as the director of nursing. I know that sounds outlandish, but it is not. It is now a well-known fact that meeting the underlying social needs of the people living in your long-term care community will go a very long way to mitigating undesirable outcomes and ultimately impact your bottom line. The people living in your communities need more than pills. They need to have a sense that "someone really cares about me."

With the increasing emphasis on the long-term care community for providing person-centered care, or as some are now using what they believe is the more appropriate term, "relational" care, (Power, 2017a), well-trained volunteers are in the perfect position to provide that level of care. Therefore, knowing how critical it is for you to meet not only the physical needs of your people but also their social and psychological needs, hiring a director of volunteers should carry the same weight while applying the same rigorous scrutiny as if you were hiring a director of nursing. For it is the combination of the director of volunteers (DOV) working in consonance with the director of nursing (DON) that will maximize the potential for meeting all of a person's needs.

What is their education and training, their experience, their work history, recommendations from previous employers, and does their personality match the job? Are they open, agreeable, conscientious, extroverted…in other words, are they a person other people want to be around? Do they have a proven passion for serving? Finally, are they able to establish and maintain a high standard for the people they accept into your volunteer program? Again, it may seem counter-intuitive to set the bar this high, but the results will be well worth the effort. Your "customers" will be happier.

Your staff will benefit as well, as they feel the lift that these "super" volunteers bring to your community. Furthermore, your staff will appreciate these "super" volunteers' valuable support. Your reputation and public image will be known far and wide, just as some of the examples I already noted in this book, i.e., Baycrest, Elizabeth Knox and so on.

Take your volunteer program seriously. See it as an integral component to the quality care you strive to provide. Yes, it will cost you something up front, but when you see your quality measures make significant improvements, i.e., fewer falls, fewer negative behaviors, your retention and turnover rates improve, and the overall atmosphere of your community brighten, you will reap great dividends on the other end. Ok, so now you have found and hired a great director of volunteer engagement, what is next?

Screen for the best, develop a vetting process.

Prior to developing a more stringent vetting process, I would recruit people to volunteer in nursing homes, having them read *Another Country*, by Mary Pipher, Ph.D. (1999) and *Compassion*, (Nouwen, McNeill & Morrison, 1983). Then I would have them write book reports on both books, and discuss with them possible nursing homes where they could volunteer. Afterward, I would call the nursing home to give them a heads-up that someone was coming their way to volunteer. I was assuming that the nursing home would vet and train them. That worked for several years until I started getting telephone calls from the people I had recruited, and they were complaining that no one at the nursing home was there to greet them or even seemed to care that they wanted to volunteer. With that, they would tell me that they were going to pursue other volunteer opportunities. As the frequency of those calls increased, I stopped the program and redesigned it by adding a rigorous vetting process and comprehensive training program that would prepare the prospective volunteer to the point that they could hit the ground running, whether someone was there to greet them or not.

Remembering the Bocks' strategy for transforming a mediocre program into an exceptional program, my vetting process started with an on-line application accompanied by submitting three letters of reference. Once those items were received, I invited the candidate to a face-to-face interview that would last about ninety minutes. An essential aspect of this process was to resist chasing after people, i.e., reminding them to submit the application or the reference letters or schedule an interview. If you are chasing people at this stage of the program, you will be chasing them for as long as they are with you.

The questions in the interview were designed not only to learn more about the individual and their motivations for volunteering, but also to see how well they could think on their feet and carry on the conversation. If the interview went well, then the candidate was invited to complete a two-day training workshop, a Friday and Saturday (held bimonthly). The candidate was required to pay $50 for the training. The thinking here was that they should have "some skin in the game" as well.

During this process, I would present several long-term care communities to the candidate for which they might volunteer, either near their home or place of employment. I did encourage them to consider some of the inner-city communities as well. Upon completion of the training, the volunteer received a certificate of completion and arrangements were made for them to meet with the person managing the volunteer program. In many, if not most cases, this was the activity director or life enrichment coordinator.

As expected, there was a high attrition rate right up front, about 60 percent of the applicants did not complete the process. However, the 40 percent that did complete the process were just incredible. While it was hard to see the stack of applications from those applicants who didn't make it through, seeing each graduating class brought great joy to me every time. They were indeed "super" people, "super" volunteers, ready to do whatever the nursing home staff would ask of them.

At Baycrest, the prospective volunteer must complete their initial training before they can apply. I've considered instituting this strategy into my program as well, as the volunteer candidate must first, demonstrate a high level of commitment to be eligible to continue the vetting process.

Creating the vetting process requires that you have clear expectations of who you want in your program. Remember, you will get what you ask for, so do not be afraid of setting the bar high. There are great people in our towns and cities looking for opportunities to give back and wanting to do it in a meaningful way. It is not uncommon for me to hear feedback from the volunteers, having completed the onboarding process, how impressed they were with the vetting and training process. It demonstrated that we were serious about our mission and serious about who will get to participate. There is nothing more damaging, however, then not knowing how to engage your volunteers. There is nothing more damaging than to have a volunteer show up only to discover that the organizers were not sure what their volunteers should be doing.

Identify what the "super" volunteer can do for you

In visiting Baycrest, (and I'm sorry if I keep referring to them, but if anyone on this planet has it right, they do), I was so impressed to see the blue volunteer lanyards worn by their volunteers who could be seen everywhere. During my four-day visit, one of the scheduled stops included visiting the morning speech pathology session. I was taken aback as I walked into a large activity room. The residents were arranged in a large circle with volunteers seated about every other chair or so. The speech pathologist was sitting with everyone in the circle as well. She would instruct the residents. Then the volunteers would turn to their partner, a resident, sitting beside them, and say, "Do this with me." Together, the volunteer and the resident would perform whatever task the speech pathologist had instructed them to do. It was amazing to see how responsive the residents were to their partner and to see that the volunteer was ready to explain the exercise and to guide the resident in performing the exercise. They were doing the work together.

But that was only the beginning of what I witnessed. Baycrest volunteers worked in nearly every department of the nursing home, to include volunteers interviewing volunteer candidates, volunteers helping with feeding, volunteers helping with crafts and arts, volunteers collecting data concerning new programs, volunteers training and supporting volunteers, volunteers developing new programs and individualized activities and the list just goes on and on.

The Baycrest volunteer candidate indicated in what area they would like to work and the staff in that area trained the volunteer for the particular task that was needed. With that in mind, one of the keys to a successful volunteer program is having staff buy-in. Once your volunteers are vetted and receive their initial training, turning them over to the staff for further training goes a long way in creating a successful partnership between the paid staff and the volunteers. The staff initially will need reassuring that the aim is not to replace them with unpaid workers, but rather to discover what tasks the volunteer can take on that will give meaningful support to the paid staff and to the residents.

Create the list of possible areas of volunteer involvement by conducting staff meetings to poll them as to how volunteers could be of help to them or use a survey that is easy for them to complete and return to you. From there you can publish the results and begin recruiting volunteers that will not only provide companionship for your residents, but will provide a helping hand for your staff as well. In the beginning, it is not an easy process for sure, but the outcome is well worth the effort. In talking with administrators of nursing homes who instituted robust volunteer programs where, in some cases, some of the staff were resistant to the idea of volunteers learning how to help them in their jobs; I asked these administrators how they dealt with this, and their answer was just, "…they are no longer with us."

As important as it is to identify specific and meaningful roles for your volunteers to fulfill, it is equally essential that you work to integrate the volunteer and paid workforce fully, to remove that "us and them" mentality and move towards the "us" only sense of community. Additional training may be necessary for both staff and volunteers to understand that we are a fully integrated workforce made up of professional staff and volunteers working towards a common goal, i.e., the care of our residents and affording them an enhanced quality of life.

Developing and implementing your training program

Developing a training program takes a lot of thought and planning. It starts by asking yourself and your team, "What do we want our volunteers to know? What should they be able to do? What skills will they need? What should they not do?" For me, it was clearing my calendar for several weeks and having access to a lot of large sticky paper, a lot of empty wall space and a lot of color sharpies, not to mention several people working alongside me to create the initial outline for the training. Also, I polled long-term care staff, i.e., administrators, directors of nursing, activity directors, life enrichment coordinators and nurse aides, to learn what they believed would be useful for a volunteer to know. This process, in total, took about ten weeks, working almost exclusively on developing the outline for the training, the objectives, and each training module. When I felt the development of the training was in the final stages, I circulated it through the long-term care community for comment.

I firmly believe that the training needs to start with giving the volunteer the context in which they will be working. For example, in my training program, I begin with demographic information: Who are the people living in nursing homes? What does the future look like for long-term care? What is meant by the phrase, an aging society? What are the challenges associated with staffing" and finally, where does the volunteer fit into the picture?

The numbers and statistics may be a bit overwhelming for the new volunteer, but it gives them an idea of how critical their role is in providing support for the nursing home residents and staff. For example, I discuss social isolation and how deadly it is to the person who is experiencing those feelings of disconnectedness, loneliness, and uselessness. I draw comparisons concerning how various cultures treat and care for their aging population and discuss how the populations of nursing homes will change moving forward in this century, requiring the volunteer to be knowledgeable and sensitive to cultural differences and requiring them to be culturally competent.

From there, I move on to introduce them to the world of long-term care. I discuss how the nursing home is organized, the various departments and functions, and how they relate to one another, how they communicate with one another, and how they support the people both working and living in the nursing home, as well as how they help the families of their residents. Then we take the "walking tour" of the nursing home, meeting and talking with staff, asking them questions about their role and observing how the prospective volunteer interacts with the residents and staff. On, rare occasions on this tour, I've had to counsel with a volunteer

who might be getting cold feet or feeling that this volunteer opportunity is more than they expected.

While the volunteer trainee is not going to necessarily remember everyone's job, or all the various levels of care, at the very least,
they will have some familiarity with the different terms they will
hear while in the long-term community. The tour may mitigate
some of their feelings of being overwhelmed by the complex nature
of the nursing home and its day-to-day operations.

It is an absolute necessity that one of the training modules deals
with the stereotypes and myths surrounding older adults, aging,
and the aging process. How many people, including professional
staff, believe that depression is a normal part of aging, or memory loss is a normal part of aging? I am not referring to forgetting
where my keys are, but not remembering what my keys do. There
are about twelve of these topics, and each one should be addressed
in the training, so as the volunteer approaches a resident, they have
the correct mindset and perspective as to that older adult's experience and their needs. The last thing you want is a volunteer using
"baby" talk and believing that your residents are living their "second childhood!" Also, by correcting their thinking, the volunteer
can be more creative and innovative in the kinds of activities in
which they engage the resident. Now that they know older adults
can continue to learn new skills even in the nursing home, they
may be able to teach the residents a new language, use new tech-
nology or most importantly, understand that even in the nursing
home, people still have opportunities for personal growth. I have
the trainees identify sources of this misinformation, most notori-
ously, television, printed publications and social media. Learning
to recognize these misconceptions and correct them goes a long
way to exposing and combating society's ageist attitudes.

From demographics to the environment to stereotypes, communication skills are the first of the practical helps that will en-

hance the volunteers' experience. What are the necessary communication skills that volunteers should have? Is it ok to shout in an older adult's ear if they are having trouble understanding what is being asked or said? Or are there better and less damaging techniques? I give the volunteer trainees a brief lesson in acoustics and discuss how sound travels to demonstrate these principles. Once the volunteer understands the essential components of good and appropriate ways to communicate, we move on to explore the skills necessary to interact with people experiencing aphasia.

Through role play and teaching the volunteer how to observe and create meaningful paths for communications, the volunteer becomes the key to unlocking the person living with aphasia. How frustrating it must be to have lost one's ability to communicate and how relieved one must feel now, having the opportunity to express one's feelings and needs because someone, a volunteer who has been trained to discover new ways of communicating, is opening that door of expression for them.

Finally, there is the subject of accountability. In this area, I cover HIPAA regulations, Resident Rights, and the volunteer's responsibilities to the nursing home (reporting hours, dress code, etc.), identifying and reporting abuse (there is a protocol that starts by reporting any suspicious behavior to their immediate supervisor). Identifying and reporting abuse is critical to cover in some detail, as the new volunteer may misinterpret an interaction between a staff member and a resident who, for example, may be hallucinating.

I end the day with a "Wrap Up" where the volunteer trainees, through activities and written assessments, review the information presented throughout the training session. Finally, the new volunteer receives a certificate of completion followed by class pictures.

When several people go through this training, a cohort is formed, "We went through this process together!" I encourage the creation of these cohorts as they create a built-in support system. I encourage them to get together to share stories, (observing HIPAA), share ideas for individualized activities, and to give them the opportunity to air their concerns. If they are working in a specific department, such as speech pathology possibly, the volunteer has learned new communication techniques that may be helpful for other volunteers to know. All in all, I want that volunteer to feel valued, well-prepared for their volunteer experience and having a sense of accomplishment for completing a rigorous onboarding process. Likewise, I want the care staff to feel at ease, knowing that this "super" volunteer has been well-trained and is ready to learn more from them.

Finding "Super" Volunteers

One of the first facts of life you encounter when establishing your volunteer program is that recruiting volunteers is a full-time job and not for the faint-of-heart. In my 26 or so years of experience, I soon learned that there were very few audiences that I would not speak to about the need for volunteers in nursing homes. In fact, to the best of my recollection, I never refused an opportunity to present the need for volunteers. The youngest audience that I spoke to was a Sunday school class made up of preschoolers. I remember standing in the front of the group of children who were seated on the carpeted floor in front of me, with their bright little faces beaming. Maybe they thought I was going to give them some candy or some other prize. Also, the children's parents were standing in a sort of semi-circle in the back of the room. I knew that even if the pre-school children didn't quite understand what I was presenting, I was confident that the parents would understand. I had hoped the parents would act on my invitation to become volunteers.

I started by asking the children, "How many of you are driven to school by your parents?" Quite a few hands went up. I then asked them "How many of you had your parents forget to pick you up after school?" To my surprise, again, quite a few hands went up. I looked up to see that the parents were a bit uncomfortable at that point and I imagine they were wondering where I was going with this line of questioning. Looking back at the children, I went on to ask, "How did that make you feel?" The children began responding with words like, "afraid," "angry," "alone," "...I was worried something happened to my mom." Then I said, "Imagine feeling that all of the time." I went on to explain that people living in nursing homes are likely to not have friends or family visiting them and that they could become "family" to the people living in these places. Both the children and the parents got the message loud and clear and from that encounter, I was able to recruit several of those families.

Recruiting is a full-time job that requires a fearless, passionate person who is innovative and can clearly, in understandable language, articulate the need for volunteers in nursing homes. Recruiting volunteers requires more than an ad in a newspaper or an e-blast. It requires that human-to-human encounter filled with stories that relay the need as well as the rewards of volunteering. Part of my message always includes the reference to nursing homes as a "library full of living books." For me at least, this is no exaggeration as I have learned, and am still learning for that matter, so much from the people with whom I spend time.

Avoid the temptation to lay guilt trips on people or to use images of poor broken down people slumped over in wheelchairs. That motivation is not lasting and will not attract the caliber of volunteers you want. Instead, attracting "super" volunteer requires first hiring a "super" director of volunteers and their personality combined with their skills will go a long way to attracting people who are highly motivated, self-starters, passionate about serving older adults and possess the capacity and desire to learn new skills. They are out there, but they are not going to respond to a program that looks mediocre and is led by a hesitant amateur. Great programs attract great people.

Your recruiting materials, brochures, website, and other social media need to reflect your commitment to the volunteer program. From there, your onboarding process needs to have that same level of professionalism that reflects an authentic desire to provide the very best for the people living in your long-term care community. At some point and repeatedly, the volunteers that I recruited, screened, trained and placed came back to me to say how much they appreciated the professionalism, the rigorous screening process, the intense training, while feeling valued and being in a position where they can now make a real difference. "Super" volunteers are looking for meaningful opportunities to serve.

Managing and following-up with your "super" volunteers

The great benefit of recruiting "super" volunteers is that there is little or no attrition, due in part to the rigorous screening process. If you are consistent, you will have established a culture of excellence in your volunteer program from the top down. One of the great benefits of "super" volunteers is that you have recruited and established a team of innovators. As a result, "super" volunteers will likely be offering ideas to you and your leadership for new activities, improvements for certain functions, and so on. Now that I've said this, I also emphasize in the training that they are to be "team players." They are not there to inspect the nursing home, but rather to work towards becoming a valuable and trusted asset to the administration and your staff. As an example, one of our volunteers contacted the administrator and requested a meeting. When the administrator arrived, there were several of our "super" volunteers gathered in the meeting room. Somewhat surprised, she asked the volunteers, "What is it that you need?" Their response to the administrator took her by surprise and was completely unexpected. They said, "No, we are here to find out what you need!" This is the difference that the "super" volunteer makes for you. So now you not only have a group of great people who are having a positive impact on the people living in your community, but you have a group of "thinking" people to whom you can turn for ideas. So, beyond the onboarding process how do you keep this program supported and "well-fed?"

One of the attributes of the "super" volunteer is that they want to continue to learn. They want resources and support that will allow them to grow in their volunteer role. Again, this is a full-time job, as the volunteer manager must be continually looking for and evaluating ongoing training content. However, the "super" volunteer will not be satisfied with the initial training. They want to grow in their volunteer experience and so follow-on training should always be available to the volunteers. Some areas to consider might be advanced communication skills, becoming a feeding assistant, creating individualized activities for people living with dementia and so on. The internet is a great place to research topics of ongoing training.

In addition to ongoing training, new volunteers should be mentored by experienced volunteers. Because of the caliber of people, you have recruited, this will be a practice that your "super" volunteers are likely to embrace readily. As with any new situation, there is a certain amount of uncertainty and a period of learning and acclimating to the culture and routines of the community. Each community is unique, as well, so the culture of each community will be unique. Having that veteran volunteer nearby raises the comfort level and eases any initial anxiety that might be present during those first few days of a new volunteer. In addition to assigning a mentor, the use of social media is important, of course, being mindful of protecting the personal health information of the residents. Various social media platforms can be used to share ideas, words of encouragement and to ask questions. The volunteers should feel included in the "big picture." The volunteers will get to know your residents very well, and so they should be included in the care planning process.

Also, scheduling informal get-togethers that include music, refreshments, possibly including a guest speaker will help to create that sense of belonging that volunteers want and need. During these gatherings, the director should recognize volunteer accomplishments. My experience has been, when asked, the "super" volunteer will say they do not want the recognition. I do talk with them, however, and tell them that the attention is not only to lift up the recipient but to encourage the other volunteers towards excellence as well. Again, this is a further argument that your volunteer program should be well-thought out and include not only a rigorous onboarding process, but also meaningful and ongoing support of the volunteers managed by a trained volunteer manager. In addition to the volunteer get-togethers, the director of volunteers should schedule personal visits with the volunteers, giving them the opportunity to talk about their activities and to voice their concerns on site.

My intent in this chapter is not to give you a step-by-step instruction, but rather outline some of the underlying principles to creating and maintaining a great and effective volunteer program that will have a measurable impact on your quality of care and the quality of life of your residents. There are a lot of great resources available to volunteer managers through groups like e-Volunteerism[21], and your local universities that detail how to create and maintain a sustainable volunteer program. My purpose is to convince you that your volunteer program is worth the time and investment, even in these days of tight purse strings.

---

[21] e-Volunteerism is one of many resources that are available to you to help you develop and/or strengthen your volunteer program. They are found at: https://www.e-volunteerism.com

CHAPTER TEN

Considering the Future

―――――

*"Change your life today. Don't gamble on
the future, act now, without delay."*

—SIMONE DE BEAUVOIR

YOU MAY HAVE read Simone de Beauvoir's *"The Coming of Age,"* (1972) In her book, she explains that societies try very hard to hide, "old age," as it is a point of "shame." Similarly, W. Paul Jones[22] observes in his article "Aging and Desert Spirituality," (2000), that we take our elderly to the edge of the desert, push them in and then get on with the rest of our lives. The desert then becomes a place of redefinition for the elder now pushed into that desolate and dry land. There, the older adult must learn new ways of living and surviving. With this mind, and trying not to be too pessimistic, I think how ageism remains so embedded in our society, that there seems to be little hope of change without an intentional and committed effort to increase community involvement in lives of the people living in nursing homes. Television, movies, and

―――――

[22] W. Paul Jones is a retired professor of St. Paul School of Theology and author. After having five daughters, he became (eventually) both a Roman Catholic Priest and a monk of the Trappist Order. He lives in the hills of Missouri, working with those in poverty and those on death row.

social media continue to propagate the same old and tired negative stereotypes of aging. Comedians make the older adult the brunt of their humor portraying the older adult as an off-balance, stumbling, out-of-touch, toothless fool, lacking any capacity for understanding the world around them. With that said, it saddens me to think how we have these "unwanted" and "unlovely" people living in long-term care institutions, tucked neatly away from the rest of the population, hidden, out-of-sight from the rest of society. After 25 years of visiting nursing homes and talking with the people that live in these places, I know that they have so much to offer if we would give them the opportunity.

Looking ahead, I find myself straining to see any signs of a changing mindset when it comes to aging and older adults. I am not all that hopeful that our society's attitudes about aging and older adults will change all that much over the next three or four decades without an intentional and well-planned effort to increase community involvement. So, it is with this book that I make my most potent argument for increasing community involvement in long-term care. For, it was through volunteering in a nursing home that my paradigm shifted, and I don't believe that my experience was all that unique. As I talk with people who are in the business of caring for older adults, I am always amazed, and I think it is more than coincidence at how many of them started as volunteers as well. So, what was it that happened to cause my head not only to turn and to not only adopt and embrace a new perspective on aging and older adults but then go on to devote the rest of my life advocating for the older adult? What was it for those people who started as volunteers that inspired them to embrace careers in long-term care? I can't speak for them, but for me it was my initial visits to the nursing home and visiting with the people that lived there, that I experienced something profound in the exchanges that took place. It isn't easy for me to articulate, but it was a profound sense of connectedness as if I was looking through time and not just looking to the past but looking to the future as well. I felt as if I had come to a sacred place where I could touch and be touched very deeply. I realized that in my efforts to lift someone from the gutter of loneliness and wanting to show them that I cared about them, I felt that I was benefitting far more from these visits than they were. I eventually began telling them so, saying to them, "I think I need you more than you need me." I know that they needed me, too, to feel that sense of connectedness, and from the smiles and tears, I am sure they did. But I couldn't deny the uplift I was experiencing. Many times, I have gone into a nursing home to make visits feeling exhausted, only to leave hours later refreshed and re-energized.

Most importantly, whatever stereotypes I had associated with my concept of "nursing home," and "old people," were transformed. And so, it was an innocent and naïve exposure to the nursing home and to the people that were living there that brought about the transformation in me. I am confident that this experience is not unique to me. Developing and nurturing a robust volunteer pro-gram, led by someone trained in volunteer management, I am certain becomes the catalyst for similar transformations that lead people to think differently about the nursing home and the people that live there.

If we hope to change the negative image of long-term care, and if we wish to attract new people to this field of work, then we must offer them the opportunity to experience this "connectedness." I tell people that it was an old woman living in a nursing home that taught me how to converse and nurture relationships. It was an old man living in a nursing home that showed me what in life is important, "...to love and to be loved." It was a 106-year-old woman who said to me, "You don't need to worry about that." It was through my visits with her that I learned intimacy. Again, I was "just" a volunteer.

Now I understand that with constraints on budgets as they are and are likely to become even more strangling, making a serious investment in your volunteer program may seem counterintuitive. Well, on the surface it is counterintuitive. You receive no reimbursement for the program. But what you will experience will have a positive and direct impact on your bottom line. Consider the impact of a robust volunteer program on your your employees' and residents' quality of life. Consider your public image and what a robust volunteer program says about your nursing home and the care you provide. Consider how a robust volunteer program that engages the community-at-large through a well-structured and well-managed program gives your volunteers a deeper understanding of the challenges you face every day. If they are the caring people, you have screened and trained; then they will likely also become champions of your cause. In fact, they will become your most effective means of recruiting more people. And like a domino effect, more people will come to experience that same transformation as I did and react by becoming more deeply involved.

And while their paradigm shifts, these "super" volunteers screened, well-trained and well-managed, are giving hope and dignity back to the people living in your community. These "super" volunteers, through their training, understand and embrace the concept of "person-centered" care helping you to identify those underlying and unmet needs that trigger your resident's negative behaviors, frequent call lights, and cries for help. Because the "super" volunteer has the skills through their training to discern those underlying needs and can inform the resident's care plan. The return on your investment, the ROI, is that you are helping to correct societal attitudes about aging and nursing homes while simultaneously elevating your resident's level of care and, most importantly, their quality of life. For it will be through your well thought-out and planned volunteer program that you will provide a deeper level of "person-centered" care, or more accurately "relational" care (Power, 2017a), for we know that more than medicine, people need to feel loved, to feel connected and it is the volunteer that is in the perfect position to create and model those relationships.

There is no doubt in my mind that over the next four decades the face of long-term care will change. But no matter what shape it assumes, it will still require professional care staff, and if predictions are correct, there will be not nearly enough professionals to provide that care. Faced with these workforce challenges, we cannot afford to turn a blind eye to any possible resource that has the potential to provide support. After years of recruiting and training volunteers and in particular during the time I raised the bar and expected volunteer candidates to complete a rigorous screening and training protocol, I discovered a cohort of people that had the will, the empathy, the intellectual capacity to learn new skills and most importantly the passion for serving. They are a group of people, a resource we cannot afford to ignore.

We know that over the next forty years, and some experts say for the foreseeable future, the challenges of recruiting qualified staff will be overwhelming. The Bureau of Labor Statistics reports that even if all women (this is the way the Bureau of Labor Statistics presented this statistic), entering the workforce over the next several decades were to choose to work in a nursing home, about 227,000 in all; the need for some 1.4 million workers will go unmet. Knowing this should cause us to ask what other resources are available to us. While I do not present that recruiting and training volunteers is a silver bullet to solving this issue, I do believe that we must explore every avenue to increase community involvement in the life of the nursing home. Among the goals of building quality volunteer programs should be undoing the stigma associated with nursing homes and attracting new workers. After all, that is how I got into this business.

Before 1992, the thought of going into a nursing home to play music was not even a thought to me. But it was during those initial visits that I experienced a profound and moving sense of need. It was then that I discovered a positive way to use my music and at the same time offer a few moments of joy to the people living in a nursing home. Over time, I became a student of long-term care through my conversations with the care staff. From them, I learned that every resident needed to feel as if someone cared about them. More than entertainment, they needed to feel as if someone cared for them. Over the next several years, my involvement grew deeper until I enrolled in a graduate program for gerontology. And now, I am advocating for people living and working in nursing homes. I don't believe that my experience is unique, in that, I think that many people through their initial volunteer experiences found a career path in long-term care that was challenging for sure, but that also brought them a great sense of personal satisfaction and accomplishment as well.

One of the final areas that I want to address is the policies and regulations that severely limit or even prohibit more volunteer involvement. As I pointed out earlier in this book, we may have thrown the baby out with the bathwater with the enactment of the Nursing Home Reform Act. Again, I recognize the nursing home industry was severely in need of increased regulations. But that was then. Now as we are facing the workforce challenges that may severely hinder our ability as a society to provide quality care and quality of life, it may be time to rethink those policies that negatively impact the involvement of volunteers. Consider other areas where volunteers are being used such as volunteer fireman. For example, the Red Cross, the Salvation Army, the Hospital Elder Life Program[23], train volunteers for complex tasks, to provide essential and necessary services as well as crucial staff support. There is no reason why volunteers cannot provide meaningful and critical support for nursing home staff. I will argue that if we can train volunteers to risk their lives fighting fires and responding to both natural and human-made disasters, volunteers can indeed be prepared to provide non-medical support for nursing home staff.

For those of you that are not familiar with the Hospital Elder Life Program (HELP) let me briefly describe the program. I believe that HELP is adaptable to the nursing home environment. Dr. Sharon K. Inouye of the Yale University School of Medicine and her colleagues developed HELP to address delirium among older hospital patients. Delirium is a diagnosis that describes multiple conditions that may present themselves when a person becomes disoriented. The older adult exhibits symptoms similar to a patient with dementia, however, the onset is sudden as compared with dementia similar to Alzheimer's disease.

The disorientation may be the result of the older adult's hospitalization. During their stay, they may lose track of time, become confused as to what is happening to them or not know where they are. There could be changes in their behavior along with other symptoms. The HELP program uses "highly trained" volunteers to provide a variety of supports to keep the older adult oriented as to what is happening to them. The volunteers offer friendly visits for social connections, massage, music, feeding assistance, and hydration. Now adopted worldwide, the HELP program provides a

---

[23] I purposely mention the Hospital Elder Life Program here because I believe this program would be adaptable to the long-term care environment. HELP is a program designed to reduce the incident rate of delirium among older hospital patients. See https://www.hospitalelderlifeprogram.org/

model for nursing homes to emulate. With the staffing challenges we are facing, we need all-hands-on-deck.

Advocacy groups like LeadingAge and the American Health Care Association could provide the voice that is needed to modify existing or develop new policies that would be friendlier to the use of volunteers and provide avenues for increased community involvement. In addition to these groups, the Long-Term Care Community Coalition, and the National Citizen's Coalition for Nursing Home Reform could also advocate for increased use of volunteers in non-medical supports. And while such remarkable shifts in the delivery of long-term care are being explored such as the Green House project developed by Dr. Bill Thomas, there are still thousands of nursing homes that are providing care under the same old model. With that in mind, increasing community in-volvement through expanded volunteer programming may offer the education and platform for accelerating the rate of change.

In talking with the leadership of the groups mentioned above, no one disagrees with the idea of expanding the role of the volunteer but what does come up in these conversations is that there is no infrastructure in place on which to deliver increased volunteer, involvement. My response to this is that we have to start somewhere, and we need to start sooner rather than later. In addition to modifying or creating a new policy, developing and launching a national clearinghouse for nursing home volunteer programs should be a priority.

This entity, in addition to being an advocate for increasing the role of the volunteer, could provide the infrastructure for de-veloping and establishing a standardized training curriculum for all nursing home volunteer managers to use in their onboarding process. Nursing home volunteers would have the opportunity to complete a training program on-line and receive a credential much like other players in the nursing home system. This entity would have a website where, in addition to the volunteer training mentioned above, there would be additional educational pieces as well, such as webinars, and add-on training modules.

Further, a menu of resources could guide the volunteer manager in the creation and managing of a nursing home volunteer program including resources that would guide them in the recruiting, screening, training and retention processes. Knowing that the numbers of older adults needing long-term care will only continue to grow, the need for increased community involvement will only increase, as well as the need to establish the infrastructure for promoting and supporting nursing home volunteer programs. We need to start now developing and putting this infrastructure in place.

Throughout this book, I have hoped to inspire you, to compel you, to convince you, to woo you, to encourage you to take your volunteers and your volunteer program seriously. When you take them seriously, they will take you seriously. That includes making sure that you have a trained volunteer manager in place and a well-thought-out and executed program. Years ago, I once heard someone say, *"You can't save the church from the pew."* In this case, this means that the incentive and the push for developing and enhancing strong nursing home volunteer programs that will be sustainable and effective must come from you, the leadership. In the hundreds of conversations, I have had with people, direct care workers, social workers, activity directors, nurses and nurse aides, I rarely if ever get any pushback from them. Few, if any of them reject the idea of training and expanding the role of the nursing home volunteer. It is only when I approach the leadership that I encounter resistance to this idea, and I understand why you might feel as you do.

With this book, however, I hope that I've been able to present enough credible and convincing evidence accompanied by examples of great programs and volunteers that you will, at the very least, discuss this idea with your staff. With them, please consider how this might happen in your long-term care communities and what impact it would have on your team, your residents and their families. To the best of my memory, I have not met any long-term care owner/operators or administrators that do not want to provide the best care and quality of life for the people under their care.

We can wring our hands and pace about our offices trying to understand how we will get our long-term care communities adequately staffed or how we will attract new workers. Developing a robust and productive nursing home volunteer program will not be the "silver bullet" for curing the challenges we face, but the strong volunteer program will undoubtedly be one of many tools that can be used to provide excellent care while attracting new workers. And let's not ignore the fact that many older adults are not going to retire in the traditional sense as has happened in the past. There is a rich pool of members of the Baby Boomer generation that are looking for meaningful ways to give back to their communities. They will be looking for organizations that will offer them significant opportunities and, (with emphasis) the training to go with the opportunity. How many of them could bring their skills and education to the nursing home to help with any number of non-medical and administrative chores? The Baycrest Health Sciences in Toronto is an excellent example of volunteers using their skills honed throughout their careers in human resources, training, interviewing, data entry, data analysis, accounting, program development, event planning and yes, even entertainment.

The Baby Boomer generation are educated consumers as well. They will be looking to see who is in charge of the volunteer program. Is it someone who is trained to manage volunteers? Or, is the business of managing volunteers delegated to someone that has to split their time between several responsibilities with the volunteer management piece getting pushed to the bottom of the "to-do" list?

Are volunteers being valued? How are the volunteers recognized? Are volunteers subjected to a rigorous screening process that filters for highly passionate and committed individuals? Are they being interviewed to discover their motivations for volunteering and does the volunteer manager work to see that those motivations are satisfied? Are there opportunities for the volunteer to grow, to learn new skills and to even advance to a supervisory position? The qualifications and expectations for your volunteer manager should meet the same high level of expectations and education that your director of nursing is required to satisfy. Well-thought-out volunteer programs led by well-trained volunteer managers produce significant and lasting results that will have a direct impact on your bottom line, the quality of care you provide and the quality of life your residents will experience.

Lastly, I hope that you know how much respect I have for the people that work in nursing homes. I hear their voiced frustrations as well as their voiced successes and rewards. I see the "Help Wanted!" signs in the front lawns of many nursing homes. In fact, recently I saw one, and I am not exaggerating, that was some ten feet wide, and six feet tall with huge red letters spelling out "WE'RE HIRING! NURSES/CNA's WANTED!" You couldn't miss it! I guess that was the point. And, there are not a few systemic issues that need addressing. But from those early days of nursing homes to the present day, significant and positive strides have been and continue to be made in the delivery of long-term care services. I just don't want us to miss a great opportunity to take advantage of a great resource, i.e., "super" volunteers.

I've seen the results of great volunteer programs with my own eyes, and that's why I am so confident that with some genuine effort on our part, we can create similar programs all around the country. And while, in 1987, it was necessary to institute policies and regulations to govern the operations of nursing homes, I believe it is time to reevaluate those policies and regulations that have severely limited what volunteers can do and work to develop ways to reward nursing homes for creating and maintaining great volunteer programs in their long-term communities.

In doing so, we create a conduit for intergenerational relationships. These relationships have the potential to challenge and correct the negative stereotypes of aging. These relationships present the older adult with the opportunity to share their wisdom and their life experiences, and to teach us what unconditional love means and how it feels. One of my volunteers, an attorney, when I asked him what impact his volunteering in the nursing home had had on him, he thought and said this, "I hug my wife a little more, and I talk to my children a little differently." The value of those changes goes beyond just dollars and cents; it goes to the very heart of who we are as a society.

REFERENCES

105th Congress of the United States. Volunteer Protection Act of 1997 (1997). U.S.A.: 105th Congress of the U.S. Retrieved from http://www.npccny.org/info/gti2.htm

American Health Care Association (AHCA). (2015). *Trends in nursing facilities characteristics.* Retrieved from https://www.ahcancal.org/research_data/trends_statistics/ Pages/default.aspx

Bangerter, L. R., Van Haitsma, K., Heid, A. R., & Abbott, K. (2015). "Make me feel at ease and at home": Differential care preferences of nursing home residents. *The Gerontologist, 56*(4), 702–713. http://doi.org/10.1093/geront/gnv026

Berwick, D. M. (2002). A user's manual for the IOM's "quality chasm" report. *Health Affairs, 21*(3), 80–90. http://doi.org/10.1377/hlthaff.21.3.80

Bureau of Labor Statistics (2016). Table 3. Industries with the largest wage and salary employment growth and declines. Retrieved from http://www.bls.gov/news.release/ecopro.t03.htm

Burgio, L. D., Fisher, S. E., Fairchild, J. K., Scilley, K., & Hardin, J. M. (2004). Quality of care in the hursing home: Effects of staff assignment and work shift. *The Gerontologist, 44*(3), 368–377. http://doi.org/10.1093/geront/44.3.368

Centers for Medicare and Medicaid Services. (2016). *Update report on the national partnership to improve dementia care in nursing homes.* Baltimore, MD.

Chen, P., Dowal, S., Schmitt, E., Habtemariam, D., Hshieh, T. T., Victor, R., Inouye, S. K. (2015). Hospital elder life program in the real world: The many uses of the hospital elder life program website. *Journal of the American Geriatrics Society, 63*(4), 797–803. http://doi.org/10.1111/jgs.13343

Damianakis, T., Wagner, L., Berstein, S., & Marziali, E. (2007). Volunteers' experiences visiting the cognitively impaired in nursing homes: a friendly visiting program. *Canadian Journal on Aging, 26*(4), 343–56. http://doi.org/10.3138/cja.26.4.343

De Beauvoir, S. (1972). *The coming of age.* New York, NY: G. P. Putnam's Sons.

DuPuis, S. L., Gillies, J., Carson, J., Whyte, C., Genoe, R., Loiselle, L., & Sadler, L. (2012). Moving beyond "patient" and "client" approaches: Mobilising authentic partnerships in dementia care. *Dementia: The International Journal of Social Research and Practice, 11*(4), 427–452.

Ellis, S. J. (2010). *From the top down: The executive role in successful volunteer involvement* (3rd ed.). Philadelphia: Energize Inc.

Falkowski, P. (2013). *Volunteer impact on long-term care facilities* (Unpublished doctoral dissertation). University of Nebraska – Lincoln, Lincoln, Nebraska

Felfe, J., Schmook, R., Schyns, B., & Six, B. (2008). Does the form of employment make a difference? Commitment of traditional, temporary, and self-employed workers. *Journal of Vocational Behaviour, 72*(1), 81–94.

Goulbourne, M., & Embuldeniya, D. (2002). Assigning economic value to volunteer activity : Eight tools for efficient program management for philanthropy. Canadian Centre for Philanthropy. Retrieved from http://www.volunteermbc.org/sites/default/files/pdfs/Assigning_Economic_Value_to_Volunteers.pdf

Gross, A. (1961). Why nursing homes need volunteers. *Modern Hospital*, *97*. Retrieved from http://medcontent.metapress.com/index/A65RM03P4874243N.pdf

Handy, F., & Mook, L. (2011). Volunteering and volunteers: Benefit-cost analyses. *Research on Social Work Practice*, *21*(4), 412–420. http://doi.org/10.1177/1049731510386625

Handy, F., & Srinivasan, N. (2004). Valuing volunteers: An economic evaluation of the net benefits of hospital volunteers. *Nonprofit and Voluntary Sector Quarterly*, *33*(1), 28–54. http://doi.org/10.1177/0899764003260961

Harvey, T., Coulter, S., Zublena, L., & Woodard, E. (2013). Silver spoons: Volunteers and patient-centered meals. *Nursing Management*, *44*(4), 8–10. http://doi.org/10.1097/01.NUMA.0000428192.22013.76

Heller, K. (2000). It's fear of intimacy, not lack of time. Retrieved from http://www.drheller.com/intimacy.html

Jones, W. P. (2000). Aging and desert spirituality, in *Perspectives on Spiritual Well-Being and Aging*. Springfield, IL: Thomas Publisher, (5-15)

Katz, M. (1996). *In the shadow of the poorhouse: A social history of welfare in America*. New York: Basic Book, Inc.

Kitwood, T. (1997). *Dementia reconsiderd: The person comes first*. United Kingdom: Open University Press.

Kramer, R. M. (1981). *Volunteer agencies in the welfare state.* Berkeley: University of California Press.

Lachs, M. S., & Pillemer, K. A. (2015). Elder abuse. *New England Journal of Medicine, 373*(20), 1947–1956. doi:10.1056/ NEJMra1404688

Litwak, E. (1985). Complementary roles for formal and informal support groups: a study of nursing homes and mortality rates. *Journal of Applied Behavioral Science, 21*(4), 407–425.

Mayo Clinic (n.d.) Delirium. https://www.mayoclinic.org/ diseases-conditions/delirium/symptoms-causes/syc-20371386, accessed 12/3/2018

Mezuk, B., Lohman, M., Leslie, M., & Powell, V. (2015). Suicide risk in nursing homes and assisted living facilities: 2003-2011. *American Journal of Public Health, 105*(7), 1495–1502.

Moss, A. J., & Remsburg, R. E. (2005). Changes in use of voluntary workers in nursing homes: United States, 1985 and 1999. *Advance Data,* (357), 1–8. Retrieved from http://www.ncbi.nlm.nih.gov/ pubmed/15932058

Musson, N., Frye, G., & Nash, M. (1997). Silver spoons: Supervised volunteers provide feeding of patients. *Geriatric Nursing, 18*(1), 18–19.

Nolan, M. R., Brown, J., Davies, S., Nolan, J., & Keady, J. (2006). *The senses framework : Improving care for older people through a relationship-centred approach. Getting Research into Practice (GRIP) Report No 2.*

Nouwen, H., McNeill, D., & Morrison, D. (1983). *Compassion: A reflection on the Christian life.* New York: Doubleday.

Pipher, M. (1999). *Another country: Navigating the emotional terrain of our elders.* New York, NY: Riverhead Books

Power, G. A. (2017a). *Dementia beyond disease: Enhancing well-being* (second). Baltimore, MD: Health Professions Press, Inc.

Power, G. A. (2017b). *Dementia beyond drugs: Changing the culture of care* (second). Baltimore, MD: Health Professions Press, Inc.

Richardson, W. (1921). *Theodore Roosevelt: One day of his life.* Jersey City Printing Company

Simmons, S. F., & Rahman, A. N. (2014). Next steps for achieving person-centered care in nursing homes. *Journal of the American Medical Directors Association, 15*(9), 615–619. http://doi.org/10.1016/j.jamda.2014.06.008

Thomas, W. (1996). *Life worth living: How someone you love can still enjoy life in a nursing home.* Acton: VanderWyk & Burnham.

University of Minnesota, Division of Health Policy Management, School of Public Health. *Dietary Services —Paid Feeding Assistants.* Retrieved from: http://www.hpm.umn.edu/nhregsplus/NH%20Regs%20by%20Topic/Topic%20Dietary-Paid_Feeding_Assistants.html Date: September 23, 2016

UN Volunteers. (2018). *The thread that binds —Volunteerism and community resilience.* Retrieved from https://www.unv.org/sites/default/files/2018 The thread that binds final.pdf

van der Ploeg, E. S., Mbakile, T., Genovesi, S., & O'Connor, D. W. (2012). The potential of volunteers to implement non-pharmacological interventions to reduce agitation associated with dementia in nursing home residents. *International Psychogeriatrics / IPA, 24*(11), 1790–7. http://doi.org/10.1017/S1041610212000798

Van Haitsma, K., Crespy, S., Humes, S., Elliot, A., Mihelic, A., Scott, C., ... Abbott, K. (2014). New toolkit to measure quality of person-centered care: Development and pilot evaluation with nursing home communities. *Journal of the American Medical Directors Association*, *15*(9), 671–680. http://doi.org/10.1016/j.jamda.2014.02.004

Vanier, J. (1989). *Community and growth* (2nd ed.). Toronto: Griffen Press Limited.

Vladeck, B. (1980). *Unloving care: The nursing home tragedy*. New York, NY: Basic Book, Inc.

INDEX

E

eating. *See* feeding, of residents
Eden Alternative, 38, 108
education. *See* training programs
elderly. *See* older adults
Elizabeth-Knox Nursing Home, 97, 106–111. *See also* Woodward, Jill
Ellis, Susan, 78–79
Embuldeniya, Don, 94
emotional needs, of residents, 50–52, 59, 96, 103. *See also*
         person-centered care; psychological needs, of residents
empathy, 69, 143, 147–148, 176
English as a second language, 109
e-Volunteerism, 194, 194n21
examples of volunteer programs. *See* volunteer programs, examples of
expectations, 179–180
expense, of volunteer programs, 91. *See also* ROI (return-on-
         investment), of volunteers
exploitation (of residents), financial, 46

F

faith, 133, 142–143, 163, 165, 172
family, as inspiration to volunteer, 123–124, 143–144, 153–154,
         171–172, 175–176
family, of residents
     and feeding, 42–43, 45, 66
     friendships with, 104
     input from, 56–57, 99
     and Senses Framework, 62
     as stakeholder of care, 99, 101
feedback, soliciting from volunteers, 194
feeding, of residents, 41–43, 45–46, 65–66, 85–86
feeding assistant, 45–46
financial abuse, of residents, 46

H

I

S

U

V

Volunteer Protection Act of 1997, 79–80
volunteer reform, 200–203
"Volunteer Service for Nursing Home Residents Reimagines Social Care System," 98, 98n3
volunteers. *See also* "super" volunteers; volunteer program headings
    caliber of, 142, 178
    cohort of, 189–190
    critical support, providing, 200–201
    demographics of, 89, 100
    impact on, volunteering (*see* impact, of volunteering on volunteers)
    vs income producing functions, 48
    and person-centered care (*see* person-centered care)
    potential, interview with, 123–124, 183
    qualities of (*see* "super" volunteers)
    recognition of, 154, 165–166, 194
    and relationships with residents (*see* relationships)
    reliability of, 78, 80–84, 137–139, 180
    reputation of, 25–27, 29, 47–48, 62
    in risky scenarios, 78–79
    types of, 139
    value of, financial, 88–94
    vetting of (*see* vetting process)
VSys volunteer tracking, 113

W

wages, direct-care workers, 38–39
walk-in volunteers, 81, 139
water, drinking. *See* hydration, of residents
Watt, Karen, 104
well-being, of residents, 52–53, 71, 76, 100. *See also* PLEASE© (Pleasure for Leisure Engagement for Active and Spontaneous Experiences) program
Woodward, Jill, 69, 97, 106, 180